THE POTTER'S HOUSE
Mary Borgstrom's Art & Life Uncovered

ALEXANDER ARCHBOLD

Copyright © 2020 by Alexander Archbold

Cover design copyright © 2020 by Aniseeker, LLC

Page layouts and graphics copyright © 2020 by Aniseeker, LLC

All rights reserved.

No portion of this book may be reproduced or transmitted in any form or by any means without written permission from the copyright holders.

Thank you for supporting the rights of the creative community.

Special thanks to Teresa.

The publisher is not responsible for websites or their content that are not owned by the publisher or its parent company.

Published by Aniseeker, LLC

ISBN-13: 978-0-9986390-4-8

First Edition

1 2 3 4 5 6 7 8 9

THE POTTER'S HOUSE
Mary Borgstrom's Art & Life Uncovered

A conversation can change your life, and on a cold winter morning at **ALEXANDER ARCHBOLD**'s antique store – *Curiosity Inc.* – that's just what happened. A couple came in to see if Alex would be interested in viewing some items at their mother's 100-year-old, 2 ½ story home in the small town of Provost, Alberta. Overwhelmed, the family had discussed tearing it down as it had become dilapidated after years of neglect. Not wanting to see potentially rare items get lost in a demolition, and always up for adventure, Alex decided to make the three hour trek to see if he could salvage anything from the site.

He took his old ambulance, done in the style of the vehicle in the original *Ghostbusters* movie, on its first highway trip with the intention of loading it up over the weekend with his findings. However, with the combination of the inaugural highway trip and the unfamiliar route, Alex found himself running out of gas – almost the middle of nowhere – with no gas station in sight. He made it to just about 10 minutes away from the town before his ambulance finally sputtered to a stop. Thankfully, the couple who had invited him was close by and was able to save him.

Alex followed the couple to the house where the mother had lived and worked as **a potter**. When Alex entered the house, he found a place full of the mother's memories and life, including her art. Alex tried his best to go through as much as he could that day, but he knew it wasn't enough.

The next day, as he headed for another round at the house, he had a crazy idea.

So, with blessings from his (understanding) wife and some convincing of the owners, Alex bought the house and everything in it.

Curiosity Inc.'s *Ghostbusters* 1973 Pontiac Grand Ville Ambulance on the road to Provost, sans gas

JUST AS I HAVE
abilities that you have
God made man
after his own image
but each is an individual
with their own special
talents and abilities
as the snowflake (said to be no two exactly alike).

TO THE QUICK GLANCE OF
the naked eye at
snow like a blanket
covering fields or
the falling flakes there
is no discernible difference.

IT IS ONLY WHEN YOU STUDY
each minute particle
with a magnifying glass
that you discover the difference
and the beauty
of each – reserving the
privilege of the Difference
so God graced us
with individuality.

**THUS THE SAME BUT DIFFERENT
YOU HAVE MANY TALENTS AND ABILITIES**

Mary Borgstrom

MARY BORGSTROM

was born in SASKATCHEWAN, CANADA on **May 18th, 1916**

to parents Charles and Jessie Mason (née Atom or Otom) and was raised in the Alberta countryside during the Depression era. She had four sisters, but often found herself wandering alone and entertaining herself. Mary eventually found a partner in her wanderings, a farmer named Marcus August Borgstrom who she had met as a teenager, and married him. Over the course of their life together, they had two children — a boy and a girl.

Eventually they moved to Provost, a small town in Alberta, Canada, in 1961. Mary was introduced to the basics of ceramics and pottery through the local Cultural Development Branch that year, but it did not take root at the time. However, in 1966, a potter from San Francisco, California named Hal Riegger visited the area and introduced Raku pottery (which originated in Japan during the early 16th century) and the method of direct firing to Mary. She also fell in love with a figurine by another potter named Maria Martinez. Attempts to figure out how to do a similar piece led Mary to exhibiting her first 'Black Pot' in an Alberta Craft show a month later. After that, she could not contain her creativity and she continued to make pieces — often venturing to gather her own clay — until she could do so no longer.

In the backyard of the house, where Mary created her pottery & ceramic pieces

Mary was a recipient of a provincial scholarship that enabled her to continue studying under Hal Riegger in 1968, which allowed her to focus on working with direct fire techniques and improving her craft. She was later one of four Canadians recommended for the Bruce Bow Scholarship in 1972, which she unfortunately lost to Karen Pascal of Montreal. Eventually, Mary grew from student to teacher and was active in teaching basic pottery courses as well as workshops all over.

Mary's pieces were shown worldwide, and can still be found in various collections throughout the world. In 1970, the Provincial Cultural Branch commissioned a travelling exhibition for Western Canada. After doing a solo show in Montreal in 1971, the Montreal Museum of Fine Arts purchased three items from this exhibition for their permanent collection. The Alberta Art Foundation purchased two more for their own collection. The Alberta Government placed samples of her work in Alberta House in Tokyo, Japan, as well as the Alberta House in London, England. And in 1976, Mary Borgstrom was invited to participate in the Arts and Culture program at the Summer Olympics in Montreal.

A portion of Mary's collection is also housed in *Curiosity Inc.'s* own store in Edmonton, Alberta, available for the public to view during normal business hours.

Brochures went out both far and wide
Proclaiming San Franciscan's pride
Make plans for Nelson throughout July
We're making pots – come do or die
A page of honours he must confess
A lot of which is plain B.S.
A sculpture of worldwide renown
But as Raku master – he claims the crown

In '66 he traveled north
to Canada to prove his worth
In Edmonton made his debut
Came, saw, and conquered as most men do
Women flocked from far and near.
Some 52 from what I hear.
His words of wisdom
Yes then on to Nelson Notre Dame
Where yearly he makes local fame.

– Mary Borgstrom

A poem dedicated to Mary's Raku pottery mentor, Hal Riegger

This refers to **Notre Dame University of Nelson** which was located in Nelson, British Columbia in Canada – not to be confused with the University of Notre Dame in Indiana, United States. During the summers, Hal Riegger held 4-week sessions on Raku pottery there. Unfortunately, the university closed its doors in 1984.

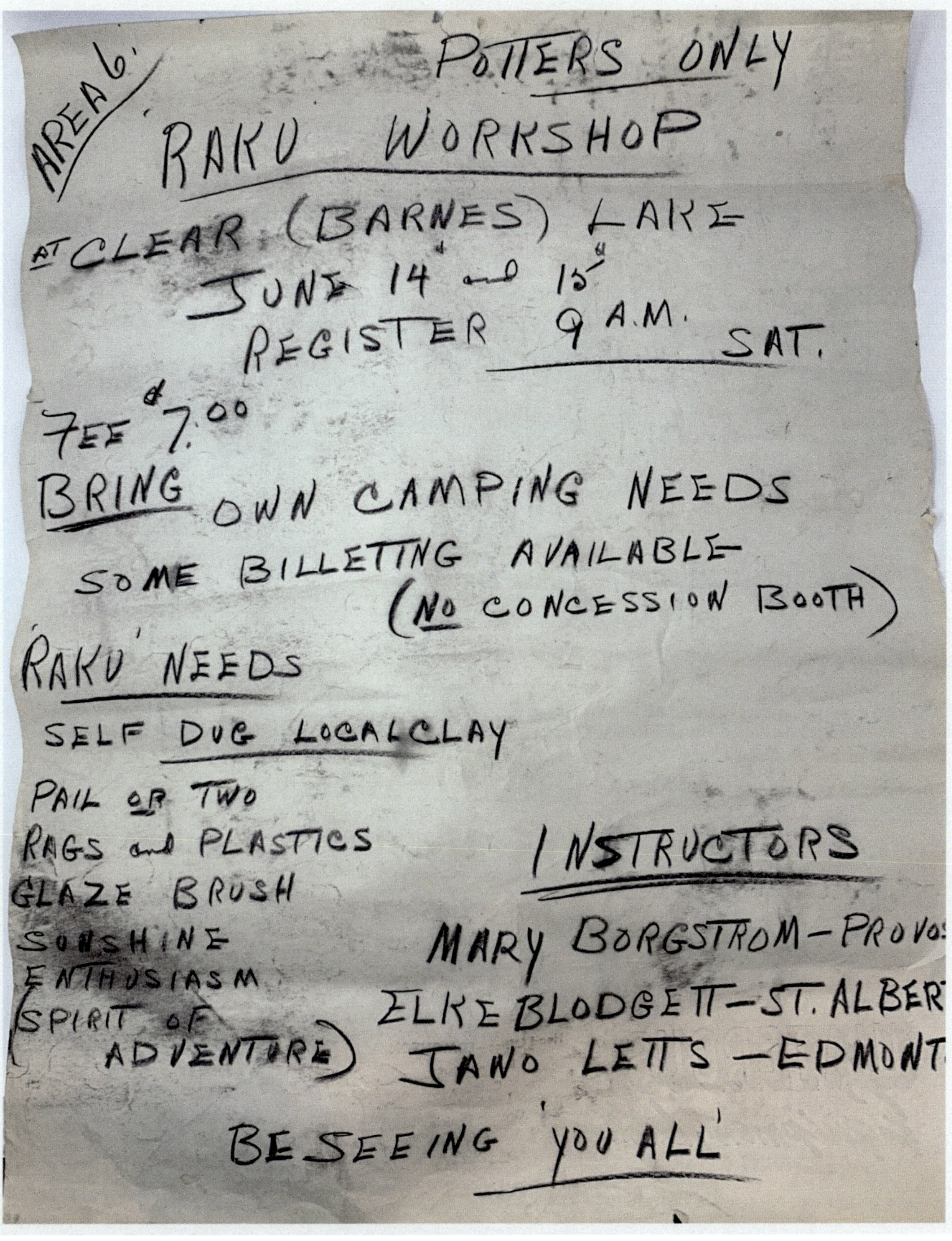

AREA 6: POTTERS ONLY

RAKU WORKSHOP

AT CLEAR (BARNES) LAKE

JUNE 14" and 15"

REGISTER 9 A.M. SAT.

FEE $7.00

BRING OWN CAMPING NEEDS

SOME BILLETING AVAILABLE

(NO CONCESSION BOOTH)

RAKU NEEDS

SELF DUG LOCAL CLAY

PAIL OR TWO
RAGS and PLASTICS
GLAZE BRUSH
SUNSHINE
ENTHUSIASM
(SPIRIT OF ADVENTURE)

INSTRUCTORS

MARY BORGSTROM - PROVOS

ELKE BLODGETT - ST. ALBERT

JANO LETTS - EDMONT

BE SEEING YOU ALL

Poster for a Raku pottery workshop with Mary as an instructor

A portrait bust of Mary's daughter.

Annual Alberta Ceramics Symposium

Mary's first piece of pottery

One of Mary's pieces displayed during the 1976 Summer Olympics in Montreal as part of the Arts and Culture program.

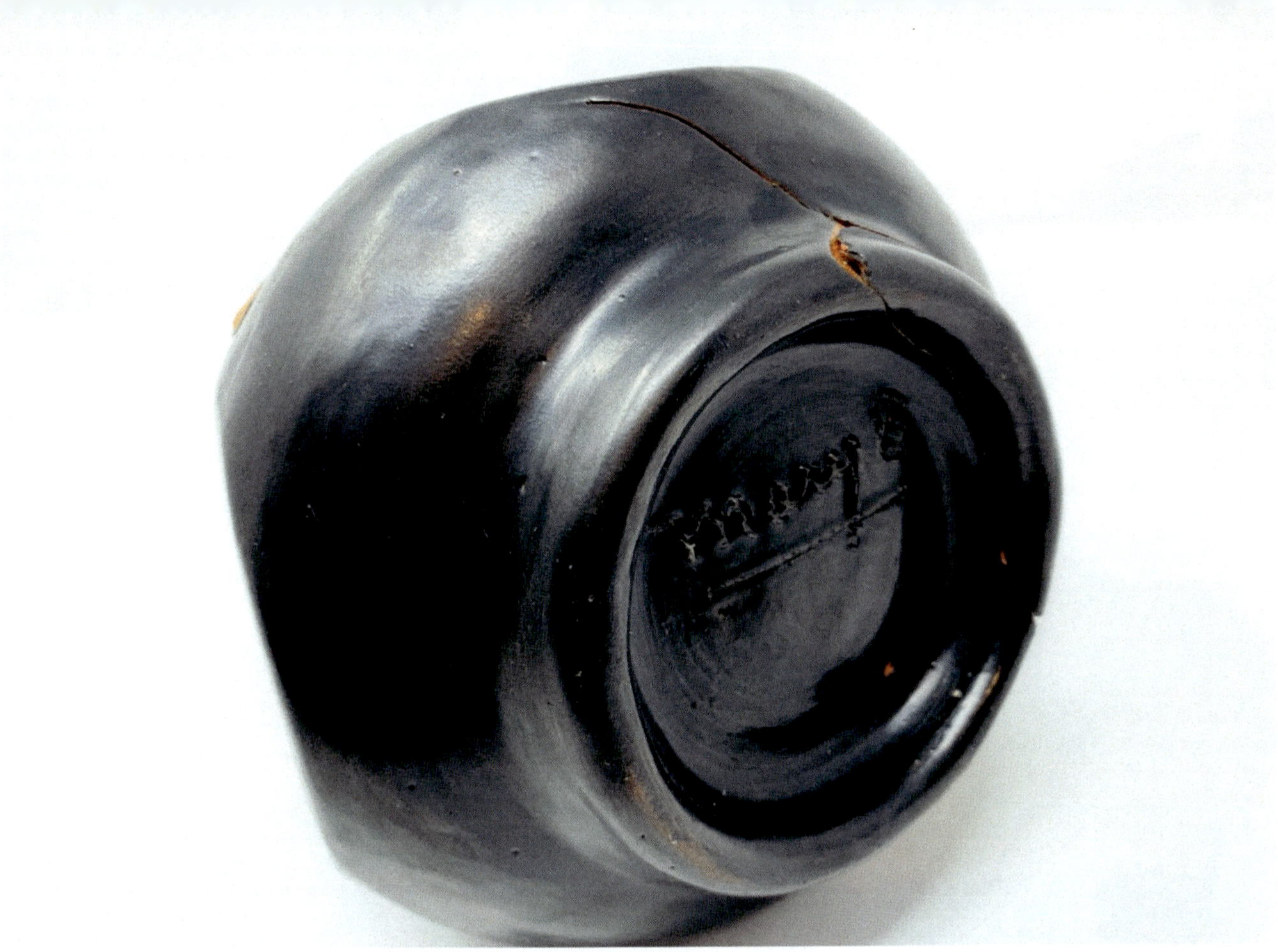

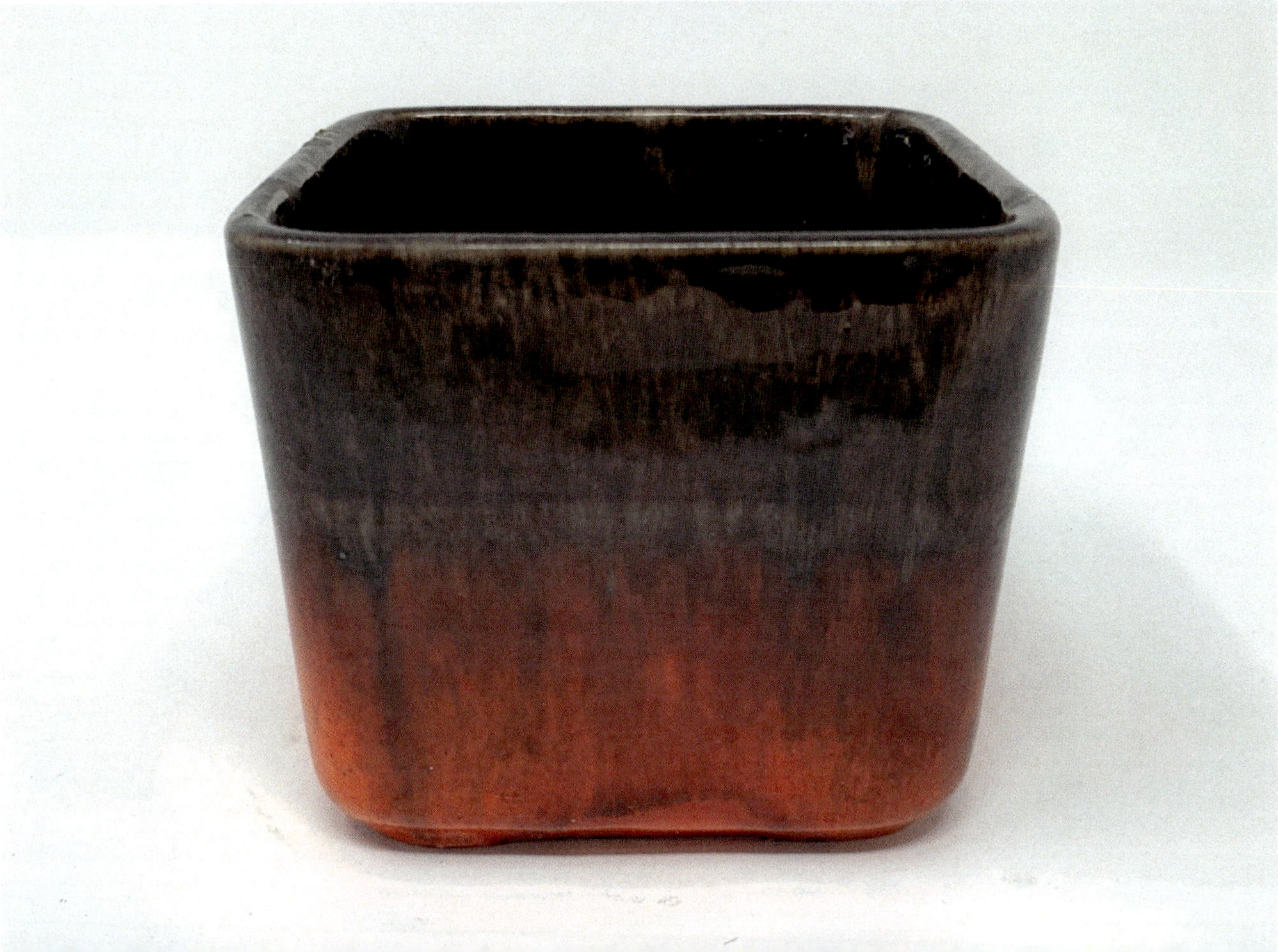

DEAR WAITING
I

Dear Waiting — I read your poem to-day
How you watched for someone to come your way
How you planned to chat, perhaps serve tea
I pictured how cozy this visit would be

How you tried to please with your special fare
How gently you set your tray just there
How you straightened your apron and touched your hair
As she sipped her tea and smiled at you
A miracle happened — you blossomed anew
Your eyes were bright — your chatter flowed
And the aura about you simply glowed

If only perhaps somehow we might chance to meet
For I too used to watch day after day
But after long years — I have turned away
    and busy myself with menial tasks
No longer important for no one ever asks
Nothing matters when there's no one to care

Mary Borgstrom

> Mary
> The clay you molded so beautifully is really you in the Hand of God.
> (... it is written forever)
> Terry

In 1939, King George VI and Queen Elizabeth of the United Kingdom toured Canada. A 22 year-old Mary penned this poem to commemorate the event.

They are coming to our fair Dominion
The King and Queen of England
Within the heart of each of us
There lies the hope to see them
The hope arises for the love
For both our King and country
And they are loved by one and all
With the British Empire
We welcome them with open hearts
May therefore it be most pleasant
May this memory of their visit
Equal that and offer our love.

Despite their Royal Cloak and Crest
They are but human beings
With hearts and blood not unlike ours
When the heart sings and when it sorrows *
They too have children such as we
And though each is a princess
Their little hearts are not immune
To parents love and kindness
We only wish they too welcome
And mingle with our children.

For where's the child that does not know
I love the Royal children.

MARY BORGSTROM

*The Royal children refers to **Princess Margaret** and **Elizabeth II** (later known as Queen Elizabeth II of the United Kingdom)*

*Text has been edited to fill in words that could not be transcribed due to fading in the original paper.

SPHERES & CIRCLES

Mary had a "fascination" with circles and spheres. She even included it in her official mark.

> **BECAUSE** I believe,
> and therefore it is my **THEORY**,
> that the **SIMPLICITY** and **COMPLETENESS**
> of the circle and sphere
> is the **BASICS** of all **DESIGN**.
>
> Others are free to argue/differ but
> – I stand firm.

– Mary Borgstrom

The stamp bearing Mary's official mark
used to imprint her pottery.

There are signs in the stars tonight
That say 'I love you!'
Even the moon high up alone
Confirms this to be true

If only you'll promise to be mine
The rest would simple be
I'll worship at the 'Lovers Shrine'
If you'd say you love me

**I love you, I adore you
Yet I only seem to bore you**

Darling can't you see
That if you'd take me
I'd lay the whole wide world before you
For it would seem to be

MARY BORGSTROM

I've always felt – believed that I/we – were so richly blessed and privileged to have you and Life. As family, Daughter and Son. We loved each of you dearly and cannot imagine our life without you.

As a girl when daydreaming about Life with home and family of my own in that Future, Someday – there was always a little girl – that I'd cherish and care for – dress like a precious doll.

A girl that was my very own.

Well! My daydreams did come true on October, 1945 when we first held you. No – when I first saw you. Before I held you – I knew – instantly I knew. And that has never changed. Not for one instant.
Oh yes! I scolded, got angry was heavy on 'Do's and Don'ts'. So many rules to follow, Restrictions, etc., etc.,

But – (as I'm sure you have sensed)
This cacophony/barrage of words and actions was all in the name of Discipline and training for Life ahead. My Greatest error or omission was not in content but in method.

PATIENCE AND GENTLENESS, GENTLENESS AND PATIENCE

I do not know which came first or if either.
They belong together – as a team. I had the Gentleness but it became buried with in for lack of Patience. Discipline without Patience becomes Harsh, lacking sensitivity and appears unfeeling.

Mary Borgstrom

My life so closely linked until there
I pen these thoughts O daughter mine
To register my heart's deep concern

Unless you tend your moods with care
Your very soul will be made bare
For all the world to look and scorn
And you will wish you had not been born
No man can like himself alone
Nor heard nor thought no ever seen
The busy world encompassed round

Along Life's twisting winding path
You have acquired a hidden path
for the very things for which you yearn

For all you render you must atone
For that which you mete out to others
Must come back in full measure
If you will search within your heart
And honestly record confessions therein
You will find a hidden treasure.

Mary Borgstrom

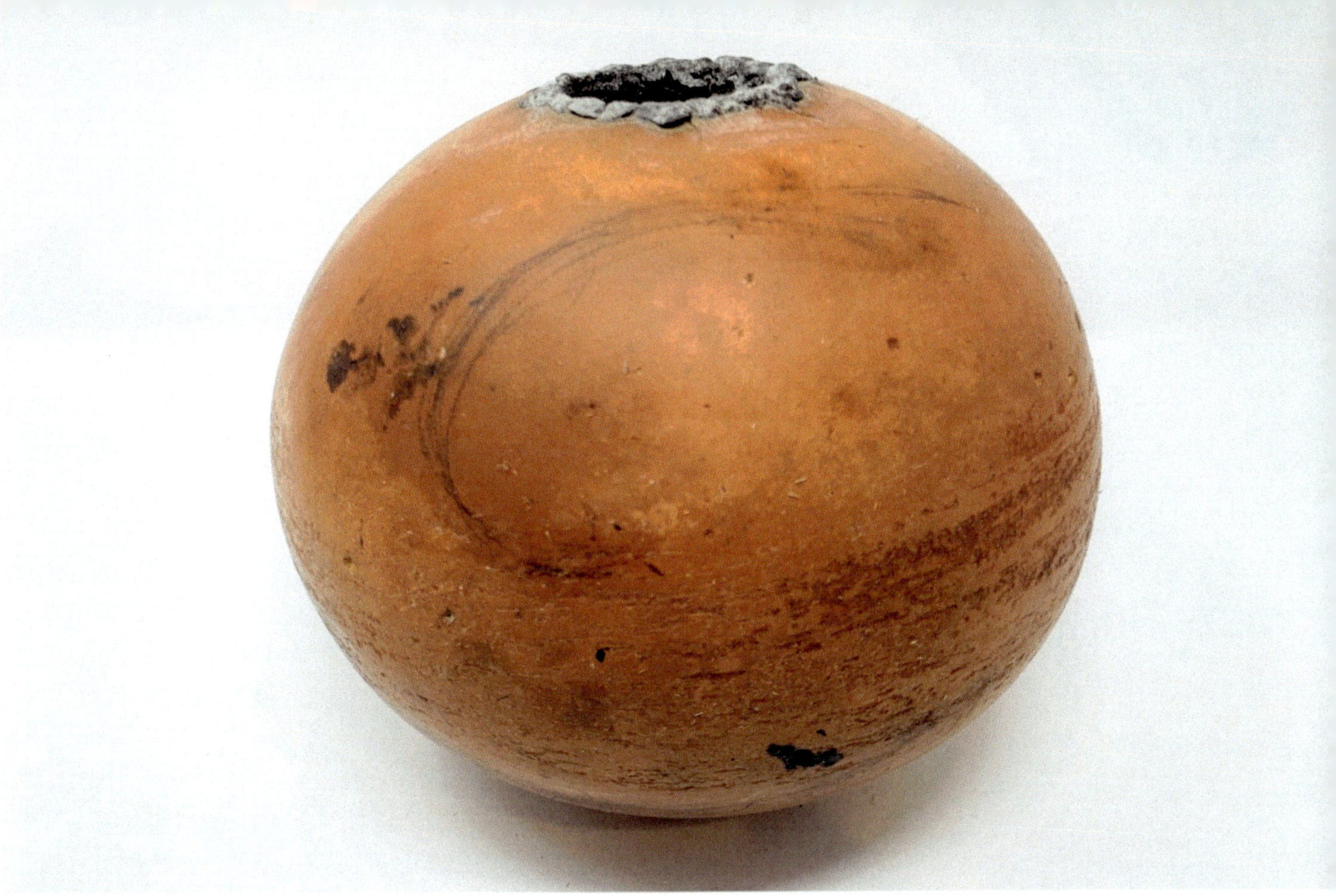
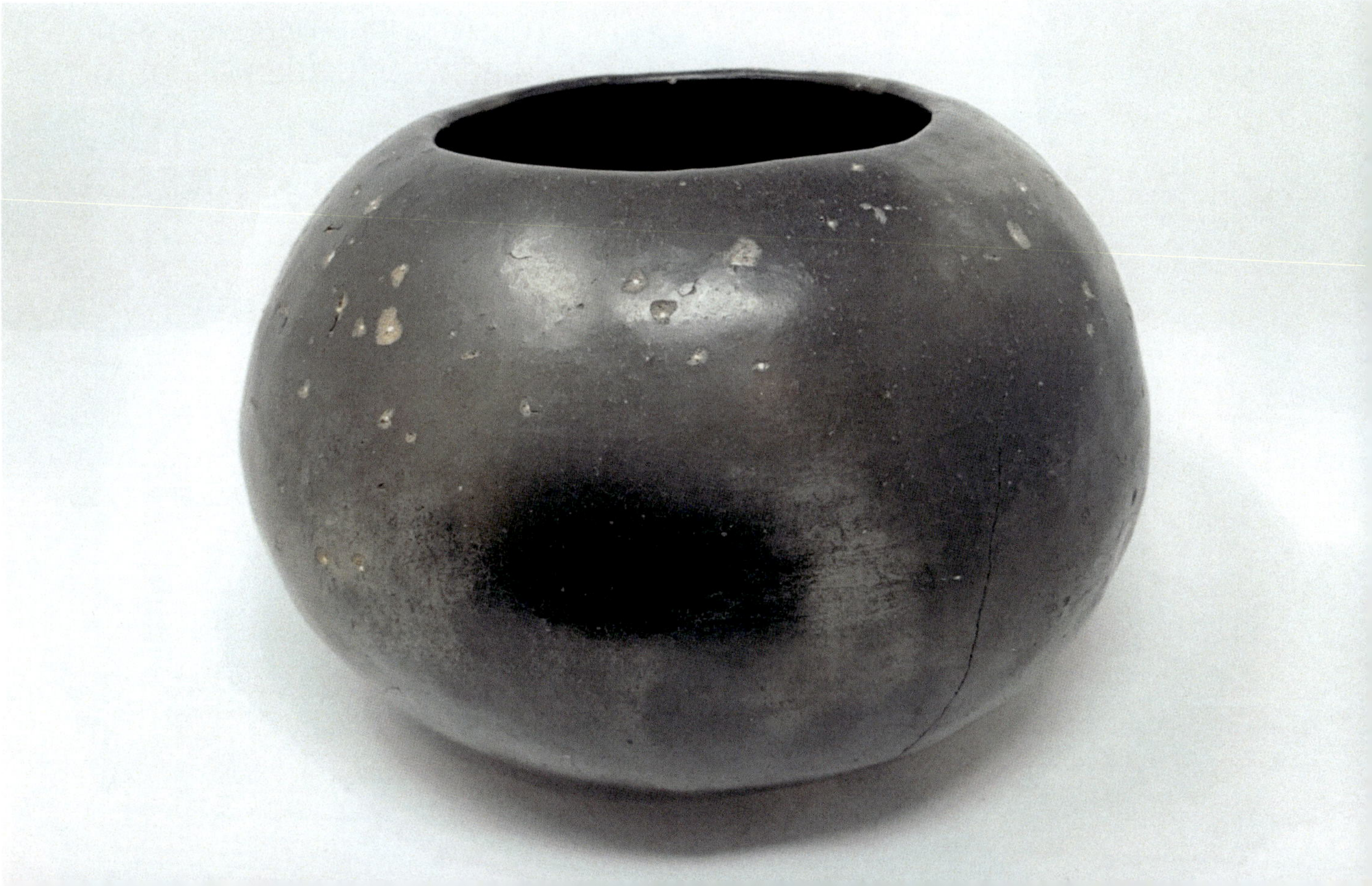

Your gestures of kindness
And your inferred faith in my talent and abilities
(potential)
An aura of wellbeing and pleasure
Not unlike a hidden treasure
Oft unveiled in secret quiet

From which I draw courage and confidence
More often than, one could ever guess
And into which I oft retreat
to renew,
and in those times of great duress

Mary Borgstrom

My heart expands in gratitude
for blessings of this interlude.
My head lifts high with modest pride
For I no longer seek to hide

You gave me strength when strength was gone
You made me whole where I was torn
Though heart — I mend body and soul
Hunger still to be made whole
Though I long with selfish regret
for dreams unbidden I'll not forget.

Mary Borgstrom

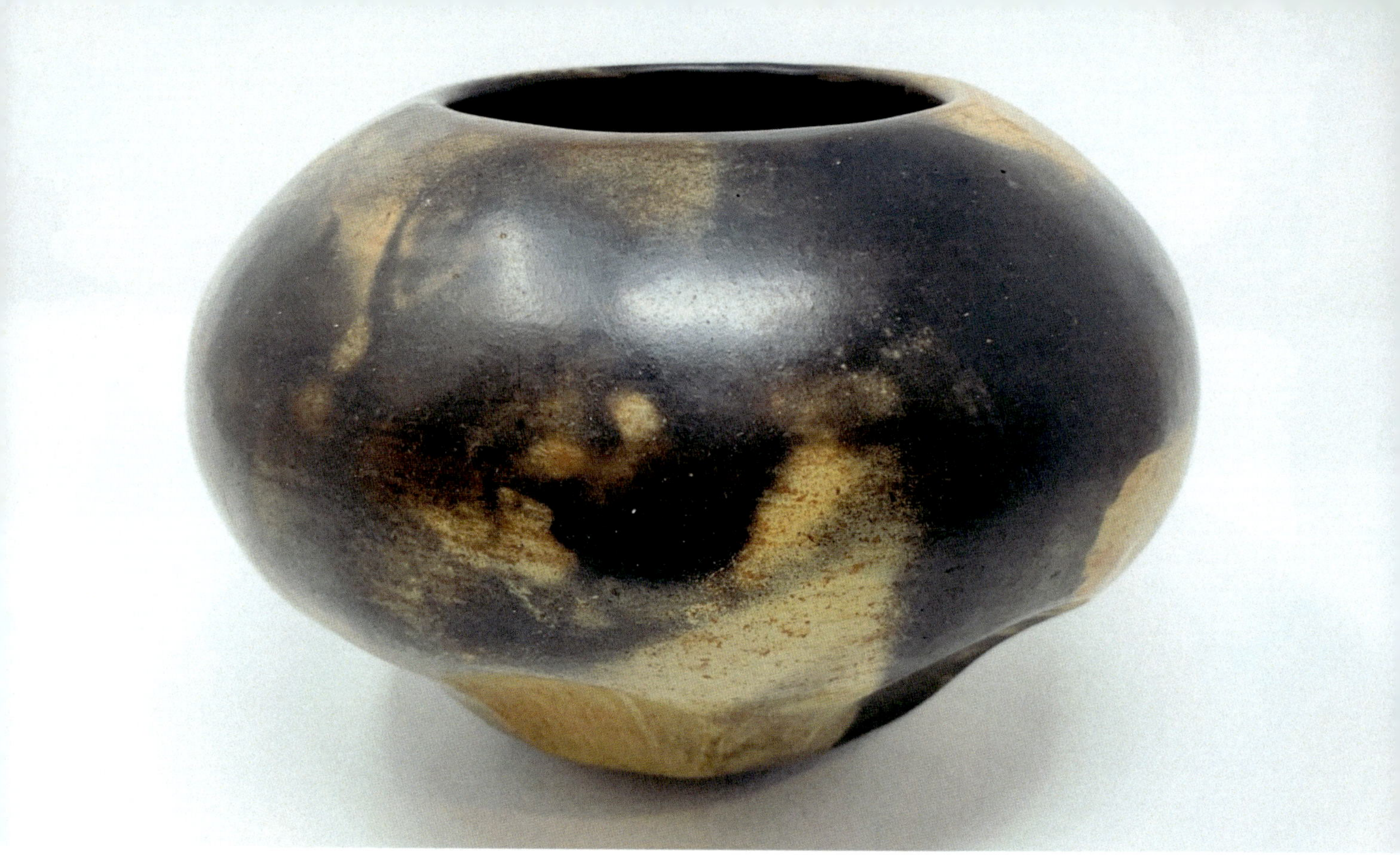

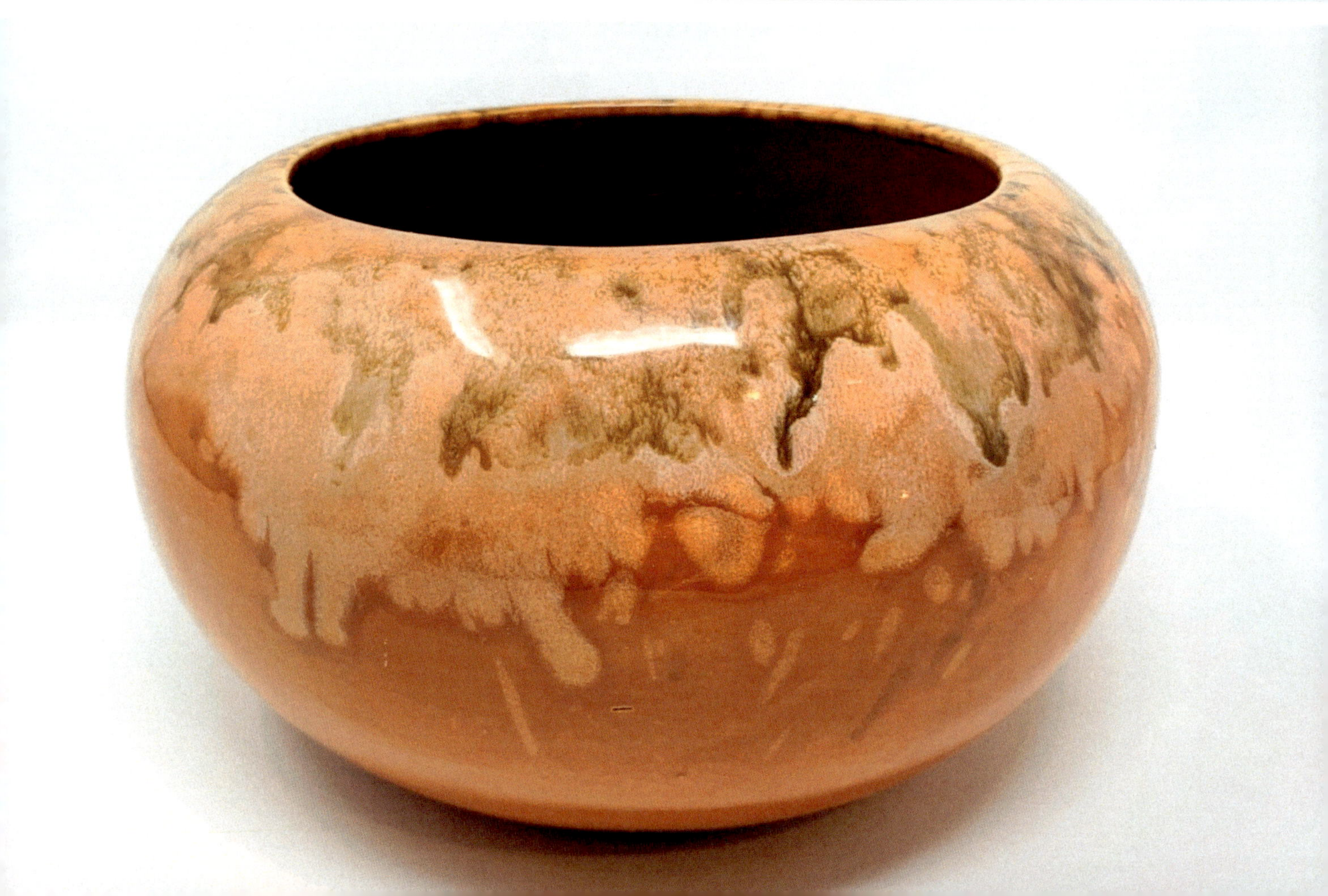

CHRISTMAS YULETIDE FOR LITTLE ONES

Curtains open in one room of home, bare but clean.
4 children poorly dressed, mother in rocking chair
Furniture consists of step ladder, stool, chair, table
(things to be used later in decorating tree).

Children say (sadly) in turn

1st: I wish we had a Christmas tree
2nd: And decorations bright
3rd: And presents and Santa Claus
4th: And an angel dressed in white

Loud knock on door
Christmas tree or child opens door

Christmas tree: Here I am – the Christmas tree
that you were wishing for
I'll be glad to come inside
Just help me through your door

(followed by decorations: 2 bells, icicle, 1 ball, 1 star)

Decorations: We're the decorations
Come to deck your tree
We will make it look
as lovely as can be

(Angel tip toes in)

Angel: I'm a real live angel
Happiness I bring
Hang me near the top
To make your sad heart sing.

(Out of the fireplace)

Santa Claus: And I'm Jolly Santa Claus
As jolly as can be
I had to come around because
I heard you ask for me.

(Followed by gifts)

Gifts: We are the gifts and presents
That you were wishing for
There's one of us for each of you
And maybe even more

Children (singing): Oh isn't this just wonderful
Our wishes all came true
Let's dance around the Christmas tree
deciding what to do

Let's put the tree right over here
The Angel up on top
The decorations here and there
And don't you let them drop

(Children hand up decorations etc.)

Mary Borgstrom

IN THE BEGINNING: MARY MASON

Mary's artistic tendencies were evident even at a young age. She expressed herself in rhymes — mostly poetry but sometimes in song. Here are a few pieces, credited as Mary Mason.

MEMORIES

Sweetheart, dear Sweetheart
        A sweet memory
        Still lingers of thee
        And of days gone by
        When you and I
        Did call each other
        Nothing other
Than just Sweetheart

Chorus

    Still to me, will you be
    The nearest and dearest of all
    Forget you! - I'll never -
    but remembering you see
    I'll wait Sweetheart, till you call.

Sweetheart, dear Sweetheart
        Remember the night
        Whilst the moon shone bright
        We wandered to-gether
        o'er field and heather
        lost it seems
        In loves dream
Just you and I, Sweetheart

Sweetheart, dear Sweetheart
        Remember the day
        The sky was gray
        You came to me
        On bended knee
        Asking release
        Thinking to cease
My love for you Sweetheart

**Mary Mason age 16
(1932)**

A song written by Mary

Darling 'tis but yesterday
   Since I bid you farewell
I would you had not gone away
   Without you it is hell.

Last night I cried myself to sleep
   Just thinking of you gone
Only to waken from the deep
   And cry again at dawn.

But sentimentalists you despise
   Is that not what you said
So for your sake I'll dry my eyes
   Then make my way to bed.

And there dear one I hope to see
   Though only in a dream
A face which is so dear to me
   With loving radiance beam.

Mary Mason
age 17 (1933)

DEDICATED TO GLADYS MEIKLEJOHN

Though time may take us far apart
And to an unhonoured end
Remember dear while I was here,
I found in you a friend
Here's hoping you, frithens your heart
Can say the same of me
And our Goodbyes
Be it but a time
To bind a 'Memory'

Mary Mason, age 17 (1934)

A friend in thought, in word, in deed
One, for whose friendship I showed greed
By claiming all the moments spare
For other friends I did not care
You are that friend oh ▬▬▬* dear
A friend who was to me sincere

Mary Mason, age 17 (1934)

*The name of the friend was not transcribed.

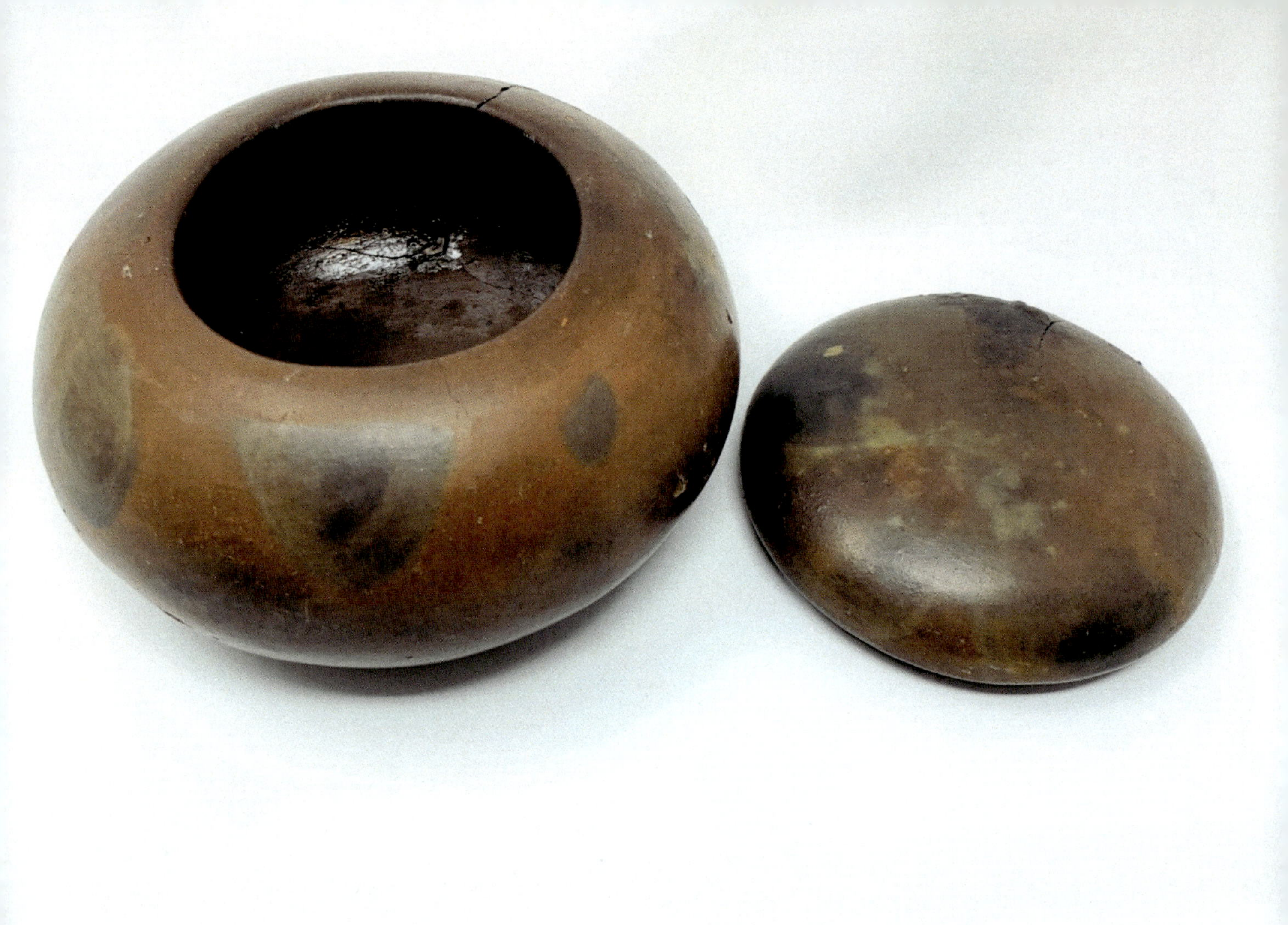

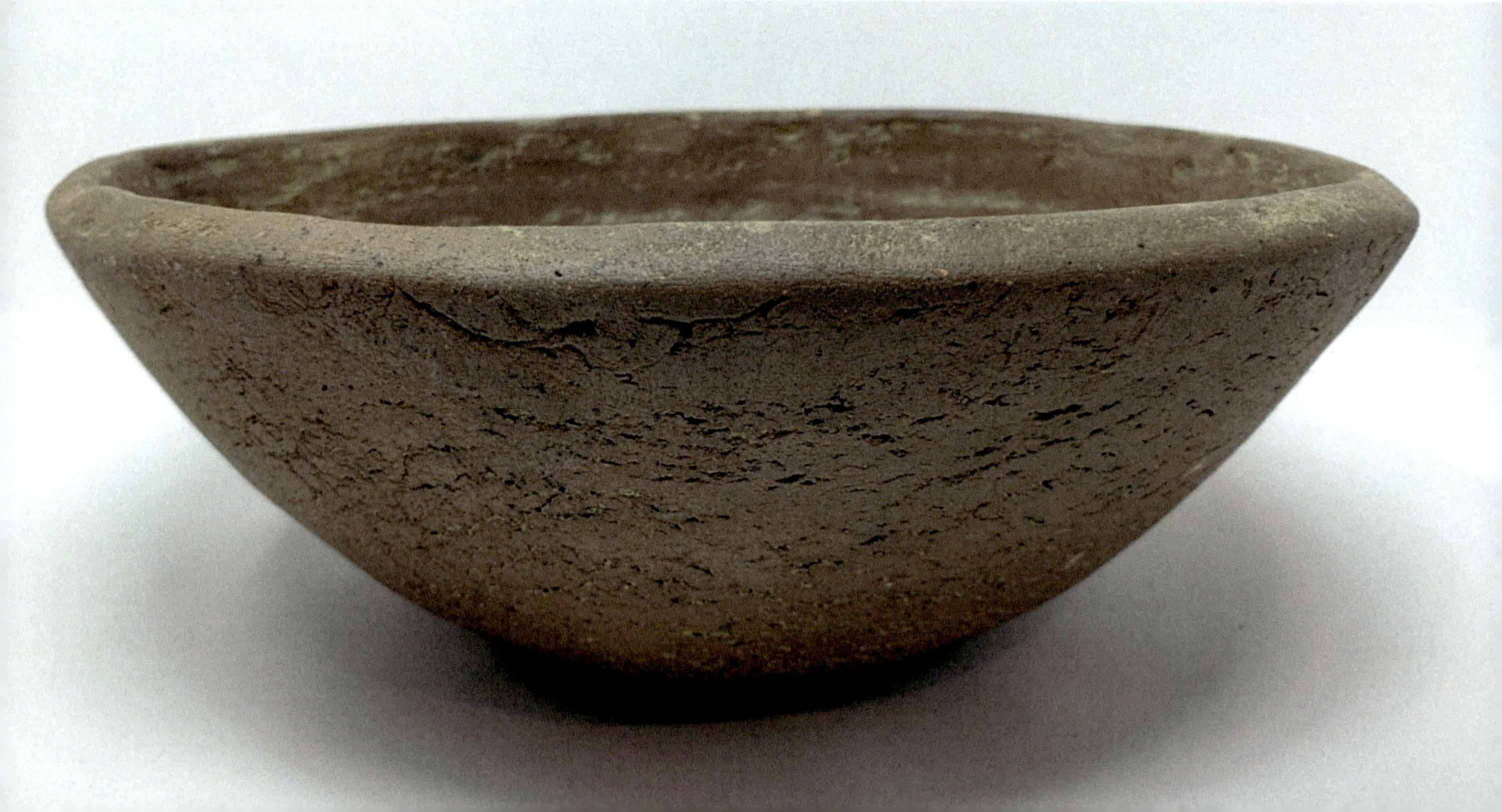

Sing me to sleep with a love song
Sing me to sleep as we drift along
Over the sea of **Happy Romance**
Love's sweetest dreams, your voice does enhance
Sing me to sleep, Sing me to sleep
Sing! Oh sing me to sleep.

Mary Mason
age 18 (1935)
(An unfinished song)

As the twilight shadows gather round
  And the stars light up the sky
Beside my window I may be found
  Watching another day die.

MARY MASON
age 18 (1935)

MARY MASON
age 18 (1935)

Deepening shadows gathering fast
a bright moon hanging low.
Twinkling stars a light have cast
Upon the world below.

As I wandered through the garden
    I plucked a golden flower
And pinned it on my bosom
    As I stood beneath the bower
Waiting for the footsteps
    of him whom I did love
For we had planned that we that night
    Should sail the clouds above.

He was a noted flyer
    But of my house a far
And though I dearly loved him
    I dared not let them know
For they would surely slay him
    Ventured he but to our door
Though the hand that would have done it
    Had ne'er done thus before.

Thus to-gether we were leaving
    My childhood home behind
And all my dear ones with it
    For, "Love", you know, "is blind".
This my one and only reason
    For wandering there alone
And my heart burned at the vision
    of a broken hearted home.

First I see them hunting for me
    Through the night until the Dawn
Then I see them find the letter
    Hastily stating that I've gone
I see dear father angry
    Whilst one look at mother's face
show the tear, so softly flowing
    When she finds I've left the place.

Alas! I cannot leave them
    Let them suffer! No, not I
T'was a cruel blow to hand out
    From the "apple of their eye"
No! I would never let them
    Suffer anguish over me
I dared not allow myself to think
    How ungrateful this would be

As I turned my steps to-wards the house
    I saw a car draw near
Whilst in my heart – I felt – the grip
    of sudden intense fear.
Out of the car my lover leapt
    and e'er I could call his name
Had made his way up the broad steps
    Waiting 'till my father came

In dreaded silence I did wait
    But father did not come
So my lover boldly entered
    Through the doors of my dear home
In silence I slipped after
    Tip toed softly to dad's room
Hiding in the folds of curtains
    Heavily laden with perfume

(unfinished)

Mary Borgstrom

Dear God I've gone and muddled things
    Just like I always do
And like a Mother's trouble child
    I bring my cries to you

Why do I do all things so wrong
    Why not the things so right
Why not accept life calmly, God
    Why must I always fight

Why can't I go along Life's way
    My hand in yours secure
Why must I always plunge ahead
    Where troubles lurk and lure

Why do I think that I alone
    Can fight the world and all
Always to find I must return
    To You to stay my fall

'Tis always You I come to, God
    When trials and troubles near
And yet where blessings come my way
    With that I ne'er come near

Dear God make me more humble please
    More kind and thoughtful be
To think more oft' of you Dear God
    and not so much of me

— Mary Borgstrom

I smiled when you said you no longer cared
I smiled though my heart was breaking
I thought of the happiness we two had shared
Since that hour of Love's awakening
But that's all over now there is naught I cared
I shall go on my way with my memories of you

Neath moon light amidst fragrant flowers
Together we spent sweet happy times
Oh its joys we two shared
But it's all over now
I'll forget you somehow
And those moments we used to call ours.

Mary Borgstrom

DRAWINGS

In addition to her pottery and her poetry, Mary also drew. Her method of drawing often gave her pieces a sort of whimsical feel mixed with elements of fantasy. Most of the featured drawings were done on the reverse side of large format advertising or posters.

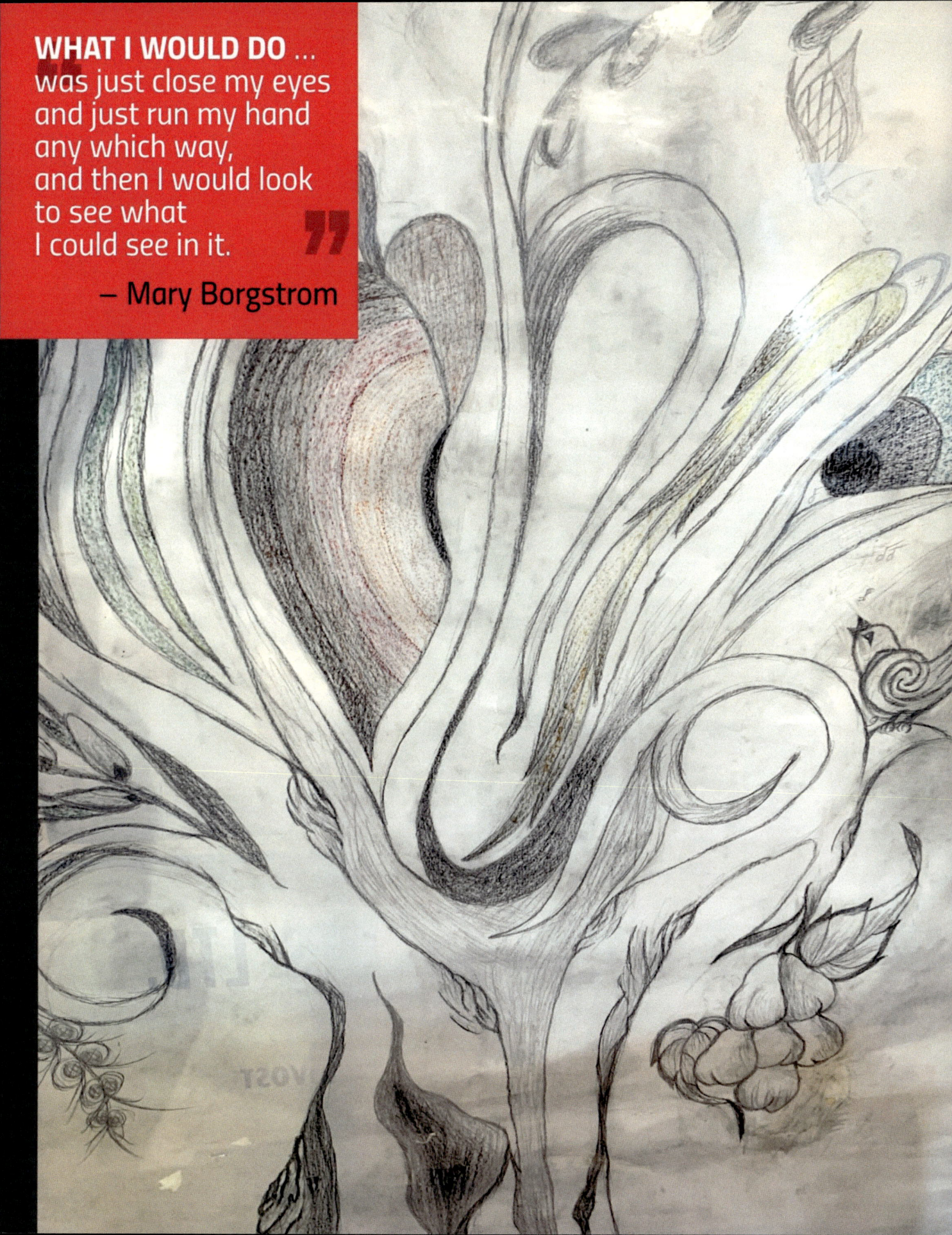

WHAT I WOULD DO ... was just close my eyes and just run my hand any which way, and then I would look to see what I could see in it.

— Mary Borgstrom

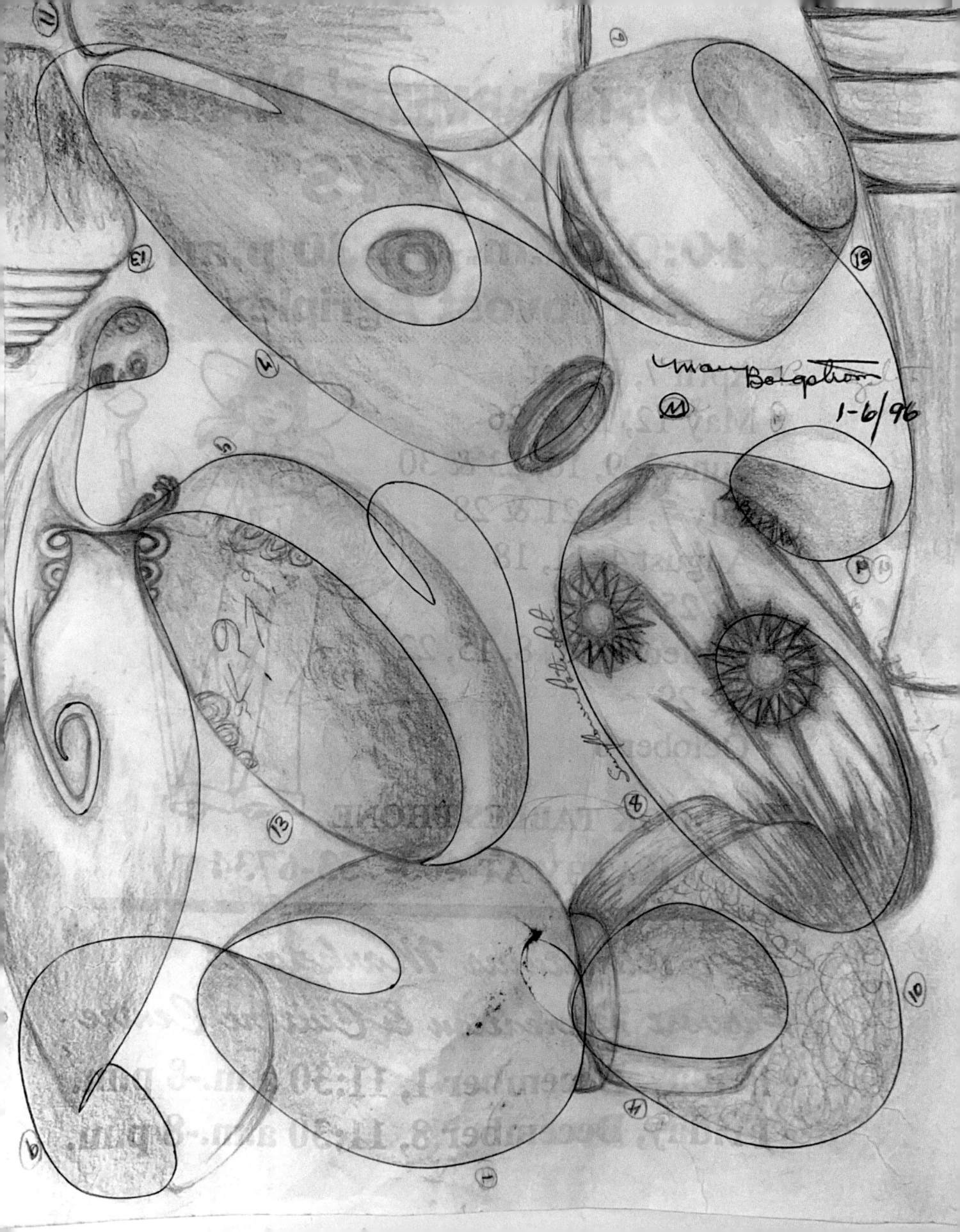

There were fairies in the woods today
Are you listening Mother dear?
I want to tell you what they said
Or don't you want to hear?

They told that if I was good
As good as good could be
And do the things you ask me to
They'd surely play with me

They said that if I went to school
And did not stop to play
And did what the teacher asked me to
They'd come again someday.

Are you listening Mother dear?
I'm sure that you are not
You're looking far away
And I know that I'm forgot

Oh now you're shouting down at me
To tell you once again
The things that fairies said to me
Down in our wooded lane.

MARY BORGSTROM

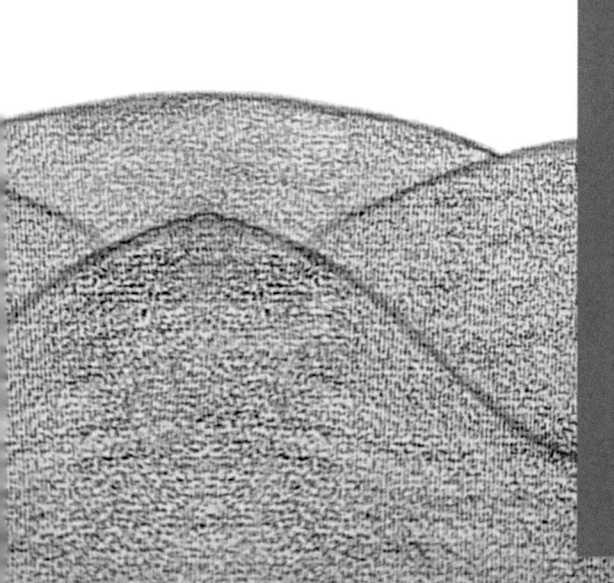

TRI-ANGLE POT — **TRIANGLE POT**

There is a land where dreams come true
It's in that land that I met you
You were so young, so sweet, so fair
The night I found you waiting there
You promised one day you'll be mine
Across Reality, throughout all time
But when I wakened you were gone
Still dreams and memories hold on

Your promise, Dear, kept hope alive
Unto the day my dream should come true
My days were long the nights so short
When in dreams we kept our rendezvous
Though t'was but dreams, I learned to know
Your loneliness to fare
Though t'was in dreams that I met you
It was those dreams I learned to care

This moment, Dear, my Dream came true
Here in my arms I'm holding you
Your loving eyes like stars that shine
They clearly say that you are mine
No more will days open endless, Dear
For always I shall keep you near.
And you and I we'll not forget
That land of Dreams where first we met.

Mary Borgstrom

DEDICATIONS

Although Mary was known worldwide as a potter, her friends and family also knew of her talent for storytelling through poetry. She was often asked to use this talent at important, personal events.

I'd rather not be asked to write
If you'd prefer the simple truth
Can one pay tribute with only words
How can a few short words pay tribute
To folks such as our Al and Ruth?

Yet they are the kind of folk
To know them at all is to know them well

Or the magic of her brush or pen

Perhaps if time was waiting not
But the hours are near at hand
To voice what my heart understands
I'd rather not attempt this task
If you must know the truth
Can one pay tribute in simple words
To folks like Allan and Ruth
For once my tongue is mute
To voice what my heart does understand.

Mary's thoughts and ideas in preparing to write for
Al and Ruth's 25th wedding anniversary celebration

Geordie and Dorothy
25th Anniversary Dedication

The Murray Boys to me were brothers
Not because I had no others,
but I was at their home so much,
I really thought of them as such

Bella and I were best of friends
There the friendship almost ends
For Robbie and John were very young
And I fought with Walter, from sun to sun.

Mabel was older – sophisticated
And already quite domesticated.
But George Alexander was kind and good
Sometimes he teased – but never rude

A quiet lad he was and dutiful
As a bairn quite Okay – beautiful
The type that's Mother's 'Pride and Joy'
This was Geordie – as a boy.

Well – he grew up – became a man
Worked hard and steady – began to plan
a life that's worthy of a Scot,
and gave the future careful thought

'Time' for the young is slow to pass
This gave him time to eye each lass.
But the local girls were friends that's all
While he search and waited for love's call.

At Meiklejohn School, a few miles west –
an Irish colleen was doing her best
preparing the students of yesterday
for solid citizenship to-day.

Dorothy Margaret Bentley, by name.
She was searching too for a 'lad to tame'.
The luck o' the Irish was in her blood,
and when they met – Geordie's heart
    went thud.

////

But soon there was a 'wee horse' waiting
Which put an end to wasteful dating.
Exchanging vows – 'I will' – 'I do'
at the Goodman home in '42

They settled down at Father's farm
with Scottish thrift and Irish charm.
And dreamed their dreams and planned
    around
the happiness, which they had found.

////

First Special event you guessed of course
a bonny wee lass and they called her Doris
What more could you ask of the month
    of May
Perfect essence of a New Spring Day.

Still further – Dorothy proved her worth
as each morning early she set forth
and walked two miles to Marquis school
teaching again, the golden rule.

Some of those pupils are here to-day
Distant green fields took other's away
and so it was thus she had a hand
in shaping the lines of our home-land.

Geordie still planned, worked hard and true,
perhaps someday to build new.
And in good time – they moved to Popes,
setting in motion, further hopes.

He planned well for he planned with joy
As he dreamt his dreams of a Bonnie Boy
who would someday walk in his footfall.
And be worthy, in time to inherit all.

Took Dorothy four years this dream to
    arrange.
Yet the best laid plans sometimes go
    strange.
And this is the part I thought was daring –
She presented him with a colleen – Karen

But Geordie was pleased and happy too
for no-one minds a girl or two.
No reason at all to get in a state –
all things are better for having to wait.

Then too there was so much to be done
To make the place worthy of a Scots' son
Dorothy kept busy with two wee girls –
P.T.A. and church and the social whirls
and W.I. – and as Geordie's helpmate –
Took them two whole years to set a
    new date.
But the day arrived – with it daughter
    Joyce
yet both seemed happy to which they
    voice

'Tis to-morrow's world we're living in
"one looks to the future and tries again".
So they carried on and chose a name
they would need at the close of their
    waiting game

He'd be named for Dad, another date set.
We figured that's why she is called
    Georgette?
It was not like Geordie to question why
He squared his shoulders and heaved a
    sigh.

For this was final – not again – not ever
More daughters to marry?! – no, no – never.
They were happy, they and their daughters
    four
Forgotten whole years there were no more

But something happened in '61
Guess a stork got lost in a July storm.
Valerie Jean Lillian was sweet as can be
They adored her so it was plain to see

And I'll bet you they wouldn't trade
For all the boys in a whole brigade.
Any way – why all this silly fun
For girls grow up as all girls must

And when they do I'm willing to bet
Each one a handsome lad will net
And soon they're as clever as Mother was –
for the future world is a worthy cause.

And each one in turned will take him home
Saying here you are Dad – he is now your
    son.
Doris already has done just this
Having entered the sated of wedded bliss
And Karen too I have be wondering a bit
If maybe she isn't thinking of it

////

But enough of this foolish fun and banter
Comparing Geordie to Eddie Cantor
It is health and happiness that counts
Not sons and daughters in given amounts.

Mary Borgstrom

Phyl & Bill England
25th Anniversary Dedication
(1941 to 1966)

Reckon you'd kinda like to know
just how they met and all o'that
and how their love began to grow?

Well now – it happened sudden like.
You all have watched a 'Lectric storm
and that there flash o' Lightnen strike.

Young Bill – he strayed from
   Bachelorhood
When home on leave at start of War.
Seems like that 'Flash' struck him
   but good.

Just three days left – that's all –
   and wow!
No time to compare notes on types
The time to marry up was now

Despite all pleadings and advice
And even plans for other dates
They chose the path of 'shoes
   and rice'

Private McLennan was asked to
   stand
In full support of Private Bill
Phyl would take on full command.

Our Bert agreed with eyes so-o sad
And trembled with unuttered sobs
"Another good guy she might have
   had"

So on the 'Eve' of found good-byes'
They gathered at the United manse
And promised to cherish until love
   dies

Now that their promise weathered
   well
Twenty and five full happy years
and gives one quite a tale to tell

Young Bill took off for parts unknown
And sailed across the angry world.
There was a war which must be won,

Phyl mooned around like some lost soul
Then fled to Tech. in Calgary
To learn dressmaking at their school

The letters went and letters came
and Phyl returned to these here parts
To play the wartime 'Waiting Game'.

Bill fought his like all brave men
Though wounded twice, he stuck it out
And stayed until the bitter end.

At last their came that happy day
When guns and hate were laid aside
And men came home – this time to
   stay

But not our Bill – this one last blow.
One foot upon the boat – "turn back
with yellow jaundice – you can't go".

It can't be true – after four years
It broke his heart to see them sail.
And he admits, he shed some tears.

But Phyl was busy as a top
Building a nest in lofty heights
above the Nagy 'Blacksmith Shop'

It was ready when he did come
for she had spent his money well
And furnished it to be a home

Bill looked around for work to do
This 'Penthouse' life is fabulous
But – sort of costs a buck or two

Well! With a panel truck – our Bill
fixed up a school bus – to become
'First' school Bus Driver – and is
   one still.

His first was the Green Glade Route
Since the idea was new and all
Folks gave the plan a lot of doubt.

But that first bus stopped only when
Replaced by bigger newer ones
And pupils numbered two score
   and ten

There came a day they bought a
   home
Though small, it was a dream
   come true
T'was great to be all on their own

That did the trick because 'ere long
A quick trip the hill and back
Brought Walter Leon – their wee
   son

Now that was really quite a scoop
Before you could count to twelve
Albert Charles had joined the group

They paused a spell for figurin'
And figured right, 'bout girls and such
Next to arrive – Victoria Lynn

Well! – by this time they were
   impressed
But thought they better just make
   sure
So – Janet Anne joined all the rest

Now they were sure and quite content
and as their family slowly grew
Found further means to pay the rent

The Bale business lost their man
So Bill stepped up a notch or two
And proved himself a good top man

Transferred in time to Stainslugh North*
A longer Route and larger bus
He sure has proved his busman's worth

Then they found their nest too small
So looked about for larger ones
To house the growing need of all

Well this here home we're gathered in
Seemed just the place for raising kids
There was nought else, so they moved
   in

Now any one could see perforce
It was too large – so what to do??
Timely solution was – of course

Betty Colleen was just the one
While all the rest were off at school
She sure kept Phyllis on the run

Somewheres 'bout here our Bill
   became
First Reserve President in town
and carried well the worthy name

He tried for business but found out
He had most all that he could do
A hauling kids on Goodlands Route

He really should have two awards
Not only married twenty-five
But also for his Bus Records.

Mary Borgstrom

---

*No record of a "Stainslugh North" was found online. This could be a misspelling, a mistranscription, or a very local term, such as "Goodlands Route" which probably refers to a business that was in the area called Goodland Energy, LTD.

George & Margaret Holmes
25th Anniversary Dedication
(1941 to 1966)

Write us a story said Dorothy to me
Write you a story! Oh no! Not me
For what can I write? What can I tell?
After 25 years they both look so well
Considerably wiser hair touched with grey
But eye's t'ward the future cometh what may

They met like all couples romanced and all that
George liked what he saw and threw in his hat
They settled in Provost and midst billings and Coos
George managed to print a 'fair' Provost News.
Margaret his helpmate kept them alive
and after a time – who should arrive –
but Georgia – their daughter – the only one
Then Ronald decided h'd better come
Then Roger and Richard – well that was enough
After all raising boys can be pretty tough
And with a newspaper there's always a deadline
So maybe George figured – this better be mine

During the war years they sent him up north
In his countries Kaki to prove up his worth
But nothing exciting happened up there
Ere long he was back to everyday care
All in all they did alright – though a fire took toll
and personal sorrows touched both heart and soul
But like all young couples – their hopes never died
Both were steeped in traditions of family and home
Which reflects in their offspring all fine and wholesome

The newspaper business kept his mind keen
And alert to all factors that he'd heard and seen.
When elected to Mayor – two terms in a row
Proved himself in that office – putting on a good show.

He stood high for integrity – the stubborn o'l coot
When this was threatened – gave himself the boot
But when you look 'round there are landmarks to see
"The proof of the pudding" – such a mayor was he

Well the years sped along — Georgia soon was a bride
Gosh! I was lucky o'l Daddy Holmes sighed
Now Alfie can have all the worry and cost
and I've gained a fine son — so what have I lost

A study Business beckoned to Ron
Perchance to show Dad just where he'd gone wrong
So off to the city for almost a year
with Ron at U.A. — he ne'er shed a tear

Roger and Richard are now leaving too
Poor Margaret was left with nothing to do
So each morning at nine she'd lock up
    and bike to the office and beg for a chore
To humour his spouse George put her to work
Which to his surprise proved she was no shirk
She took care of the office and sent out the bills
Fed them and clothed them and cared for their ills
The boys helped with the newspaper
    with picture and news
George shared with the public connections
Each Tuesday P.M. around about 4
at the local Post Office we arrive by the score
To read and to comment and yes! to complain
    and this world once we prove once again
That we are people — Common variety kind
    and George keeps on printing with never no mind.

Well they've been on a holiday
    midst mountains and lakes
We're hoping the trip was great for their sake
With Ron back from College and Margaret back home
We're expecting great change will now surely come
The weekly newspaper will perhaps become daily
    and all of the pages be festooned most gaily

But all joking aside — we are here to express
Our sincerest best wishes for your happiness
You've weathered this test for 25 years
Through trials and Error, Through laughter and tears
So do try for 50 — cometh what may
Will try to be 'round for your next Special Day.

Mary Borgstrom

Bob & Wanda
25th Anniversary Dedication

Long ago it seems to me
I knew the Meyer Family
Beulah, Allen, Lester, Maggie
Wanda wore the 'youngest' badge

The Hager family south some miles
Oft went by and exchanged smiles
Then Jack and Beulah exchanged rings
And that began a chain of things

Frank and Maggie took note of this
Saw the worth of married bliss
Sweet sixteen she was when he
Pleaded "will you marry me?"

Wanda now was left alone
With only Pa to sit at home
The Hager boys now numbered two
Bob and Orval – both she knew

They wondered this thing called love
And started like one done
And they wondered 'Gosh! Oh Gee!'
Would she maybe marry me?"

Bob in haste to beat the other
Begged 'marry me not my brother
Not knowing Orval wished to wait
Until he'd found his perfect mate

And Wanda swept quite off her bean
Said "Bob I will" at just fifteen
Yes Bob and Wanda married young
Thinking t'would be lots of fun

And so it was and so it is
But there is more to wedded bliss
For like other they did find
Bliss up mostly state of mind

You have to work for what you get
And they hadn't started yet
And so in time along came Dawn
They were so thrilled – as time went on

They thought that they should have another
Lorne – and Murray too – a baby brother
There followed Myrna, Grant and Joan
To make sure they are not alone.

They ordered Craig and Dean
A fine family time not seen
But if you think all joy they've had
There were times that were quite bad

Those few years with drought and ill
I'm sure you folks can well recall
and everyone has sickness – loss
and times when wondering who is boss.

But Bob and Wanda weathered this
And carried on in wedded bliss.
Built up their lands by working hard
Collected stock and pigs for lard

And when they found their herd too small
Then built this home to house them all
Their first born Dawn is married too
Presents a grandchild now and then

Lorna going to study more
Brings you when 'ere she visits home
Marian became his Dad's right hand
And helps to farm this fertile land

The others still are running round
Fitting the house with joyful sound
Yes Bob and Wanda married young
Thinking t'would be lots of fun

Found you have to work for what you get
And they have worked real hard you bet
And when we look at what they've done
It makes us wish we'd married young

For it may very well be said
That they have years and years ahead
To reap the harvest they have sown
and pleasure in the things they own.

And so our wish for Bob and Bride
The very best with you abide
We pray that God will richly bless
You and yours with happiness

And through your laughter and your tears
May you look back through former years
To this glad night when all of us
Mark your Silver Anniversary

And when your Golden years rolls round
You can be sure here we'll all be found.

Mary Borgstrom

Jessie Atom Mason
Dedication to Mary's Mother (1889 to 1972)

Jessie Atom the youngest of four children. Born to John and Edith Atom in 1889 in Bohina* Province then Austria (now Romania) emigrated to Canada with her parents in 1908 to join her two brothers on their homestead in Wynyard, Saskatchewan. Sister Annie remained in Austria throughout her lifetime. It was in Saskatoon that Charles and Jessie met and married and sometimes made it their home but as with many others in those very difficult times there was considerable moving about from city to country and back again. Where ever, whenever work was available.

Of this five daughters born to the Mason's, 4 living.
Mary:
    married to Marcus August Borgstrom
Phyllis:
    married to William Arthur England (Bill)
Beatrice (Betty):
    married to Donald H. Thomas, Ed.M.
Peggy:
    Deer Home (Michener Centre) Red Deer
    (Peggy was mentally and physically
     handicapped)

(In regards to work)
Charles Mason's disappointment was monumentally discouraging. He had fought in World War I for Canada, and had several years of farming experience in Canada, plus his great love of the land and its creatures. It was morally discouraging to be thus refused. However – no – one ever heard of Charles Mason bearing a grudge against his fellow man, and throughout their Lifetime – he and Herald Tipler were the best of friends.

Mrs. Mason like all pioneers of the 20's and 30's managed miraculously to keep the family clothed and fed – especially after her husband's illness. In those days grants, pensions, etc. were most difficult to come by and very frugal at best with no medical aid other than the generous heart of the General Practitioner. Excellent Cook and working the Singer Sewing Machine Jessie purchased shortly after arriving in Canada served her well both before and after marriage and family. Converting bleached sugar and flour sacks into highly acceptable garments for self and children. At age 8 made herself dresses and aprons.

Slips, another product of her nimble fingers, were gloriously enhanced with deep wide yokes of crocheted medallions or daintily trimmed with edgings of that magic art of tatting which is in fact thousands upon thousands of knots joined together with that quick silence dart of the tatting shuttle. Many, many friends, neighbours and acquaintances were recipients of gifts of this magic which she never lost. The day before her death at 82 she was tatting yet another for a friend whom she had taught to crochet almost 50 years earlier.

Mrs. Mason was a superb cook of simpler home nourishing foods, the kind that built health bodies and made one hasten their steps upon nearing distance. (Together with the most wondrous bread this side of Heaven.)

Her love and dedication to gardening and knowledge of maximum production according to kind and quality, the back breaking hardships of hoeing, and carrying of water which had to be pailed from slough or deep well paid off in bountiful produce for winter storage in dirt cellars to appear throughout the winter months in the mouth-watering meals – the sameness of which never palled the appetite. (When you are hungry, you are hungry!)

Her many skills learned in her mother country as a way of life born of necessity, would have put her in the forefront of to-day's rush in the Cultural upsurge towards Arts and Crafts. Throughout the country – indeed throughout the world – skills of which she spoke sparingly of at all: the growing of flax and wool, pinning it into threads then weaving into cloth both hemp and wool upon looms made by their men-folks, to be later sewn into garments for all. Meats to last a season, preserving of fruits and vegetables into... Oh yes! These were the pioneer skills which made our country awaken. Unfortunately somewhat reluctant to speak of it because this was the work of peasants, a necessary means to survival, and by the 20's and 30's Canada was already striving to overcome and forget such menial origins – Depression or No.

Having overcome with the advent of machines, affluence, early retirement, short work hours, theirs is suddenly surplus of idle time. Time at last for cultural needs from which springs our heritage back to originality. The spinning wheel, the loom, the basket, and quilt and fine embroidery, aroma of fresh bread from one's own oven, the wholesome foods. Back to the country quiet, the slower pace of the more primitive approach to life where one can take a moment to listen to the song of a bird or sit quietly in the stillness.

Notes:

Although this may not have been written by Mary, it contains important information regarding Mary's family and a bit of their history.

*The only 'Bohina' found online is a small town in Belarus, which is nowhere near the former territory of the Austro-Hungarian Empire (Austria) or territories of Romania. It could be a transcription error or a name in another language. Bohemia and Bosnia may be candidates as they were part of the Austro-Hungarian Empire, but neither became part of Romania. In an interview of Mary Borgstrom (conducted by Alexander Archbold), Mary mentioned that her mother was Ukrainian or from the Ukraine.

Jessie Atom was sometimes referred to as Jessie Otom.

Charles Mason, Mary's father, lived 1880–1951.

OTHER ART PIECES & ARTIFACTS

Artists, with their obvious appreciation for art, often have an art collection of their own. It comes as no surprise that Mary had many other interesting pieces of art scattered around her house in addition to her own. This section contains a few of the pieces found in the Potter's House.

> Do you know how to drive a baby buggy?
>
> Tickle its toes.   :)

A joke found written among Mary's other writings.

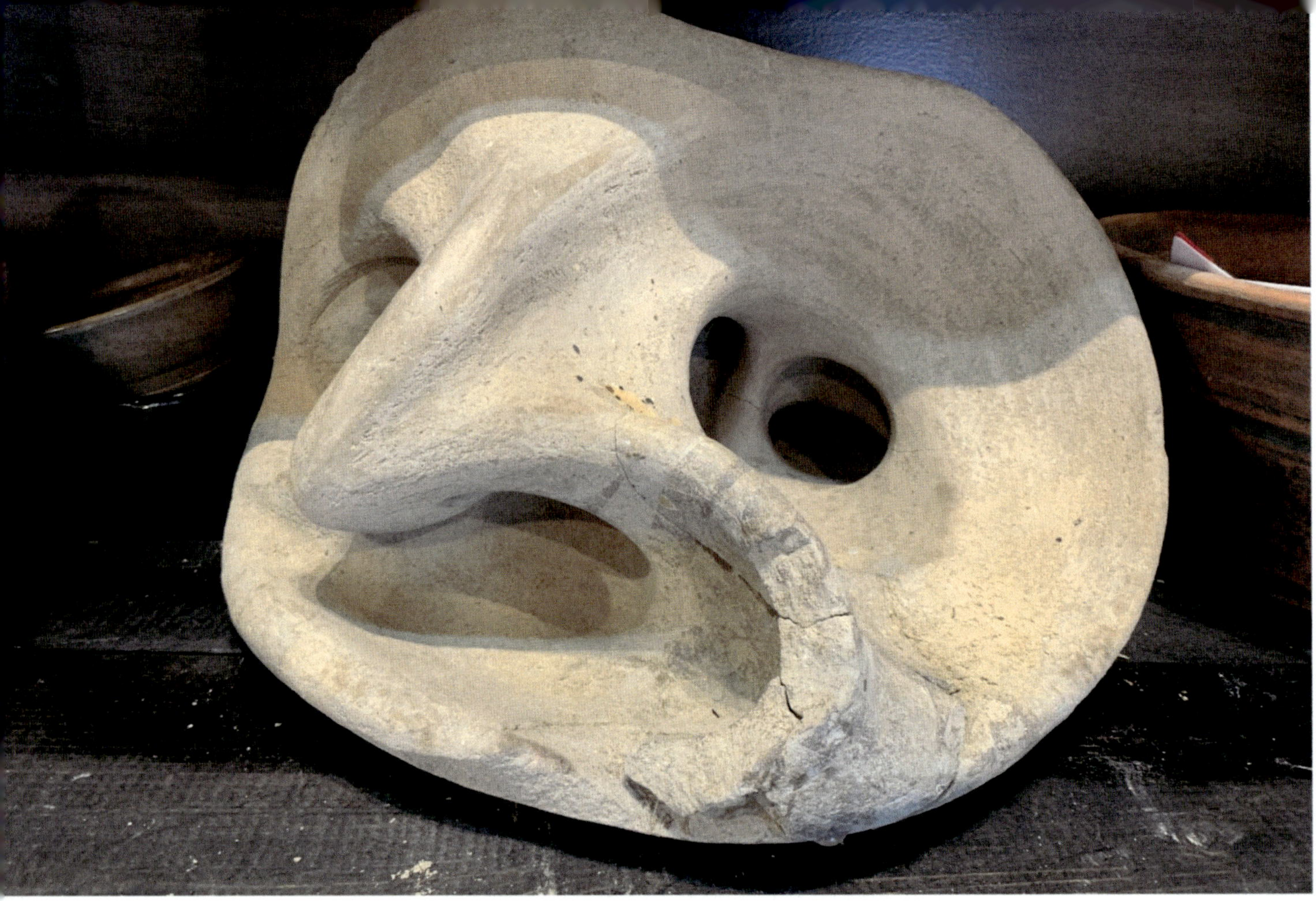

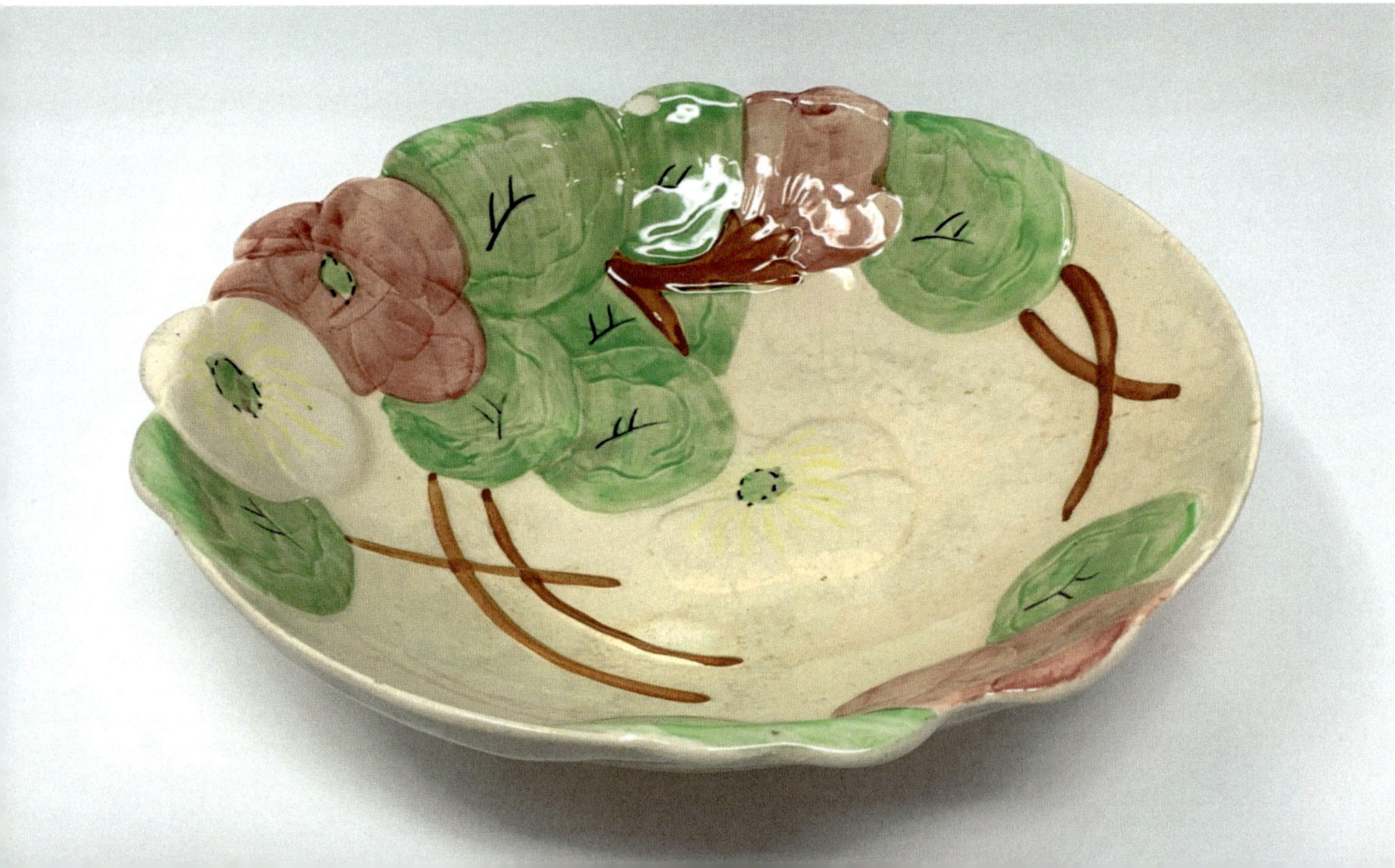

A COWBOY'S FATE

I'll tell you a story, if hear me you will
Dark is the night, all tempests are still
Not a star in the sky, not a sound to be heard
Save the far way echo of some unknown bird
A cowboy comes a riding along by the way
His head on his breast, he has ridden all day
His horse lame, he comes riding alone
And then the horse stumbles, the cowboy is thrown

Rays broke o'er the mountains soon comes the sun
Showing the world what darkness has done
He leans o'er a bolder, a gash in his head
In his right hand a letter and this is what it said

"To the world in general, this I must write
Though Death hovers near and dark is the night
Though you – too cruel to give me a grave
I can thank you at least for that which I crave

You first took my joy by taking my mother
Very soon after my dear dad and brother
And later when I would have taken a wife
Did you not undertake to stamp out her life

Did you not turn all my friends into foes
and cruelly strip me of food and of clothes
But I'll no grumble now – I'm quite satisfied
To know now that I'll wake by my dear mother's side

Yes all of my dear ones will be on the shore
To welcome and cheer me as I ferry o'er evermore
And now my strength fails, my pen, its ink dry
So world cruel and bitter, I bid thee goodbye

Text has been edited to fill in words that could not be transcribed due to fading in the original paper.

MARY BORGSTROM AS MARY MASON

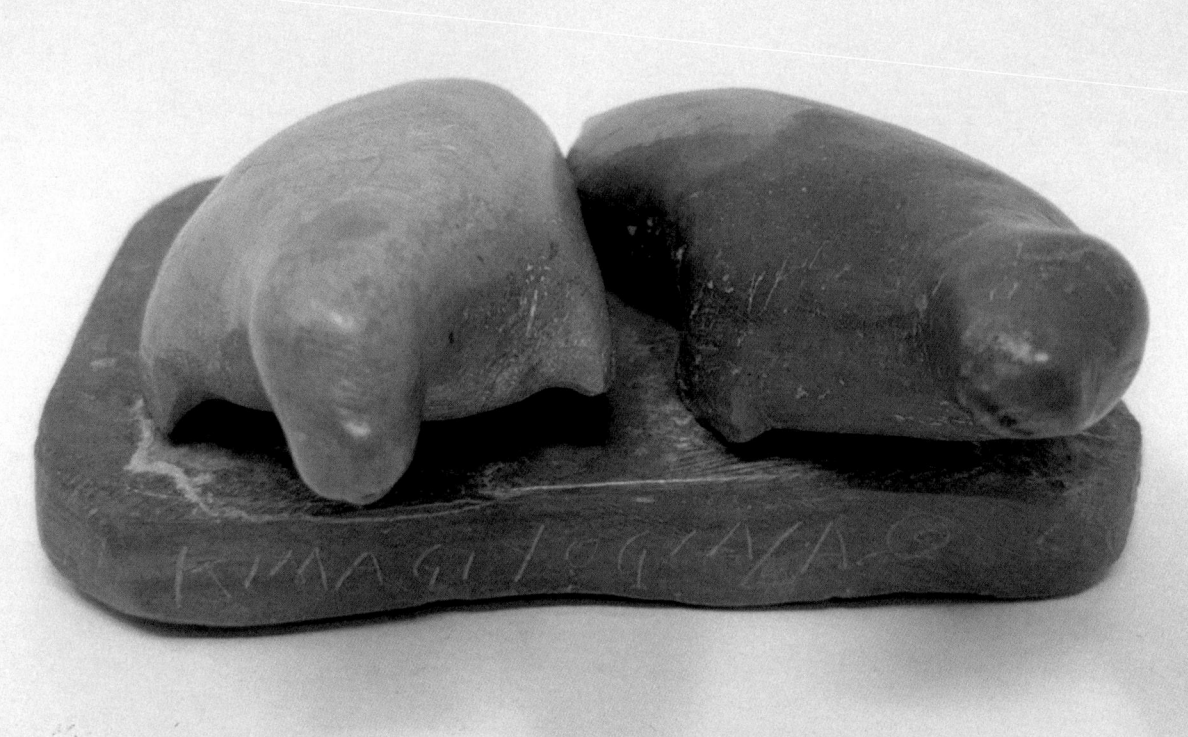

I CANNOT BELIEVE THAT THIS IS ALL
that nothing goes beyond this realm
This ship of Life on endless seas
no Captain at the helm
And if there be a Captain
Who planned such
so wondrous wise
One lifetime ne'er would be enough
to use the knowledge given
to earthlings here below
and not enough for heaven.

Mary Borgstrom

THE WEB WAS WOVEN STRONG AND SURE
Strands were strong, the knots secure
Promises became the lure
and constant hope helped to endure
The weaver wove with patient care.

Mary Borgstrom

MARCUS AUGUST BORGSTROM

Mary had met and dated Mark while they were teenagers. They were married for 59 years, and had known each other for much longer. However, in 1997 Mark passed away. For the first time in a long time, Mary was separated from her life partner – and this affected Mary deeply.

Resourceful Mark
Humble Mark, yet proud of what he had.
Rare Gift of acceptance of Life's Situation
    and circumstances

Friend to all, Envy of none
Live and let live, Doubt others his motto
Philosophical in his approach to all matters –
often revealed in his tongue and spontaneous
    sense of humour.

Private in his own Life, he respected privacy of
    others.
Philosophical by Nature. He not only would have
    made a great philosopher.

His life style simple. Though his interest and
    knowledge was expansive.
His world was his Family and all Family members.
His special love was the Grandchildren, His own
    and everyone else's.
He delighted in the life of a growing child.

Birds always true
What ever Mother Nature presented
a humble man, and honest man

There in lay his strength.

Mary Borgstrom

Carrying the load until one got their bearings
Sometimes it **worked** well
Sometimes poorly and
Sometimes **not at all**.

But along the way we learned many things
Sometimes solution of answers came readily
Sometimes it required ingenuity, inspiration
and invention to hold it to-gether until
common sense and stability returned.

The experience taught us many things
New knowledge was acquired.

Fifty-nine years and a lot of adjustment and
compromises were made **AND** still far from perfect

Now only half remains.

My Husband is gone
I will not be far behind
If you still have your Families,
Cherish and Treasure them,
Don't waste time and effort
One day, any day your tears will
will spill over, overwhelm you.

Don't leave room for regrets.

Mary Borgstrom

Like Rip Van Winkle awaking from his thousand years sleep and out of touch with his new surroundings. He finds himself in a state of uncertainty, Shock, Bewilderment, and a pocketful of Fear and Hesitancy all resulting in confusion lack of directive and Initiative, confirming and adding full inadequacy already suspected and admitted. Such rabid negativity running rampart in a mind, slowed down to shut out the world, is very debilitating to say the least – and defensive in protecting the status quo – knowing full well reasoning behind proffered physiological analysis and counselling is healing wisdom.

I wonder, and I ask bluntly, can one learn to accept so quickly the comfort of this heading pause of the soul, called withdrawal, to commit oneself to permanent residence. Or is this a temporary escape to give one space to heal body, mind and just until such time (as a child learning to walk, one step after another) one emerges out of the confining resultant cocoon of isolation and quality blends into the general flow of Life, Wiser, Richer for having been processed throughout this devastating experience of loss, helplessness, hopelessness, soul searching, self-blame, anger, frustration, bewilderment, loss, loneliness –
Round and round they go,
nonstop, over and over,
When will it end?
Where will it end.
How will it end?

It will end in Sorrow.

That is about where I'm at now and not quite – it is just beginning. Perhaps then – will come acceptance?
Until Sorrow and Acceptance arrive I guess I cannot expect healing.
Denial seems to be blocking the progression.
The Body is rested – but physically in lead shape from too much rest and under activity.
The mind is anything but rested because of one activity of self-analysis, reliving negative, dwelling on might have beens – should have beens, never can be's and never will be's.
Once in a while I get to 'this and that', might be's, could be, but once taken by the negative and I wallow through a few more rounds. When I get to 'this will be' perhaps then. I hope so.
Perhaps then the Spirit will revive and generate moral support and charge the battery of Renewal for Body and Mind. I hope so.
Meanwhile the soul has been persevering in a tug of war struggle to hold them all together through this journey under the shadow of Death.

My Faith and trust in God, Keeper of my Soul, Perhaps this is my Salvation – not only my Soul, but of whatever is left of Life here on Earth. This I believe, because even through this whole ordeal My Faith has never faltered. It became more ardent – more

dependant and trusting, more searching.
In this Faith – I know and depend on it. Is it a fear – and the Scriptures quote, "a little fear is the beginning of Faith". Whichever/whatever – it Sustains me.
So – God willing 'Let the Healing begin'.

At the moment I am just beginning to stir from the moorings after being caught in a Time Warp and undergoing solitary cleansing. From Deep Freeze to thaw can be time consuming. It depends on the climate. The angels in my stratosphere are sensitively attuned thermostat Regulators. How can I possibly fail? Now it is up to me.

I plan to live here in my house, no matter what the circumstances surrounding my Life, **until I decide** to do otherwise. This is my home. It was my Husband's home. For 37 years. He never wanted to leave it. Not even this past year and a half when for the first time he was not able to do anything except look after his 'personal needs'. I have come to the conclusion that he knew much more than he let on because he never complained other than to say – "Get someone else to do it. I'm finished with all that." Any conversation re: his health resulted in great anger and refusal to discuss it. Period.

I've known Dad since I was 13 years old. First dated when 14, together until Irene and her friend. We were married 59 years thru Heaven, Hell and back again. We built up this condemned place until it was talked about because it was a show piece. We both worked HARD all our lives. We both had much sickness, stress, and life skill problems. We got through them with God's help. We did not lean on Family/Friends. Perhaps that was a mistake. We were taught to be strong. That too may have been a mistake.
Like too much exercise in Body building or too much of anything – something has to give, some things get lost.

I am not stupid person – Not as you would. But when I have all facts or clear directions and these are possibilities I understand and can follow. If not – I know how to ask questions. Like travelling from A to Z you get and follow a mapped out route from point to point. If not you narrow it down to asking precisely how, what, where, and why, etc. And arrive at a precise door, not on a precise 50 ft. lot in Timbuktu, to greet your long lost Friend. Step by step you arrive however long it takes. I have always arrived at my destination one way or another.

But – you do have to start with that first step and sometimes it is a zero. Sometimes it is not done very well with confusion, haste – fragments and pieces of guess work and direction. It's been rammed through a time slot.

These past few days – have been just that a now and then nothing decision, time scheduled or planned.
I buried my husband, a combination Family Reunion, shock/sorrow. (worse can get more so – But – so can Better).

Under extreme stress of mind, body and soul I have been under severe stress for the past year which kept escalating to the point of sheer exhaustion. Dad and I married and became a unit of one, for richer, for poorer, for better or worse. Neither of us was perfect but together we were twice as good. We leaned on each other. Sometime heavily, one or the other. Under such exhaustion, stress, long hours lack of sufficient sleep plus age – brings one to a breaking point requiring much more of others regarding sensitivity and understanding – a touch, a word, a smile – not for long –
just until I find my way again.

You were surrounded with it within your family reunion, you had and concentrated on each other.
In the midst of all this warmth I felt cold and alone –
Yes! even frightened a little –
momentarily I am lost –
It's too soon to get my bearings –
it may take a while –
just now I depend on you –
but you have your family – I just lost mine.

        Someday – you will understand
        How can I make you understand

        Someday you will.

Mary Borgstrom

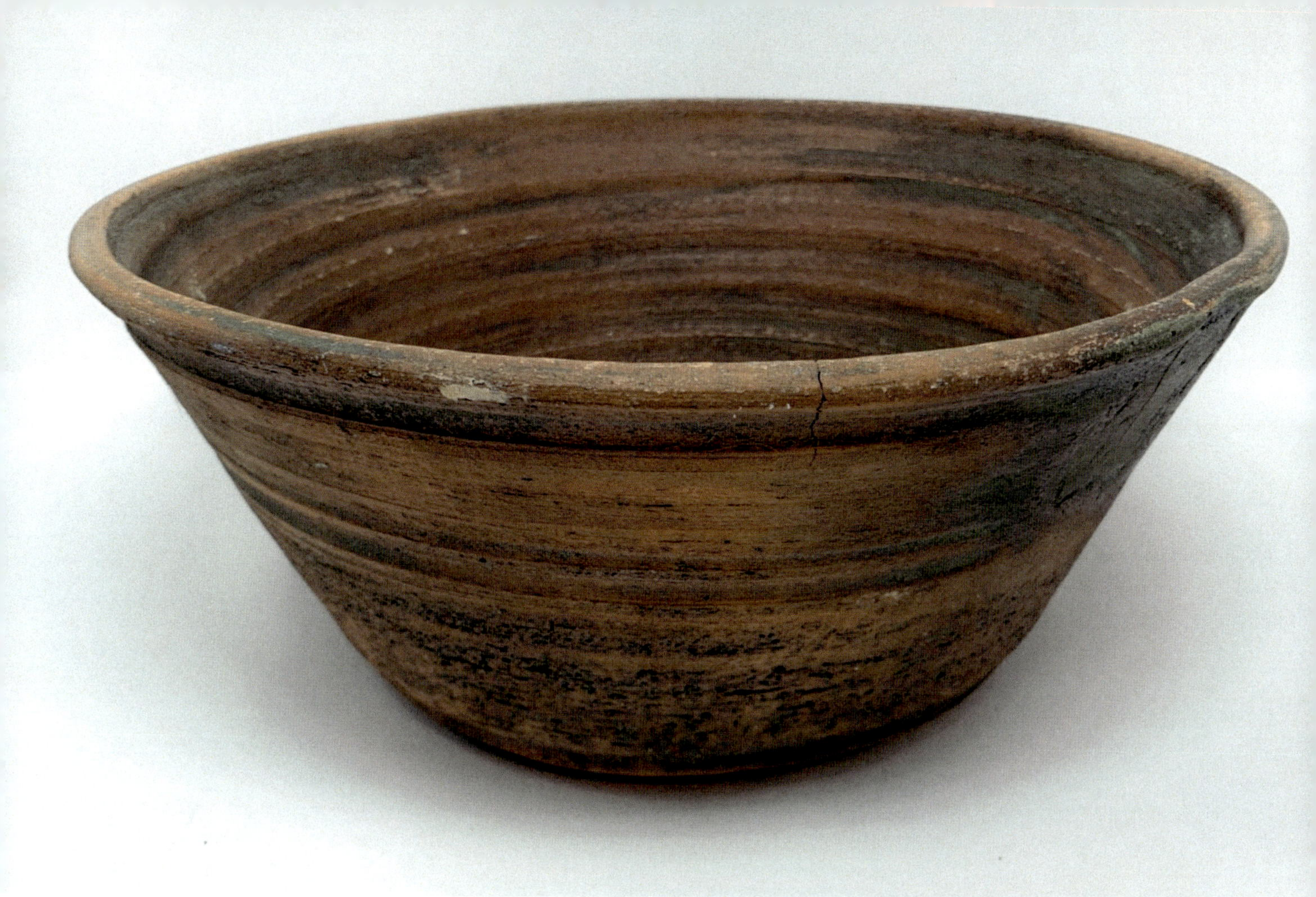

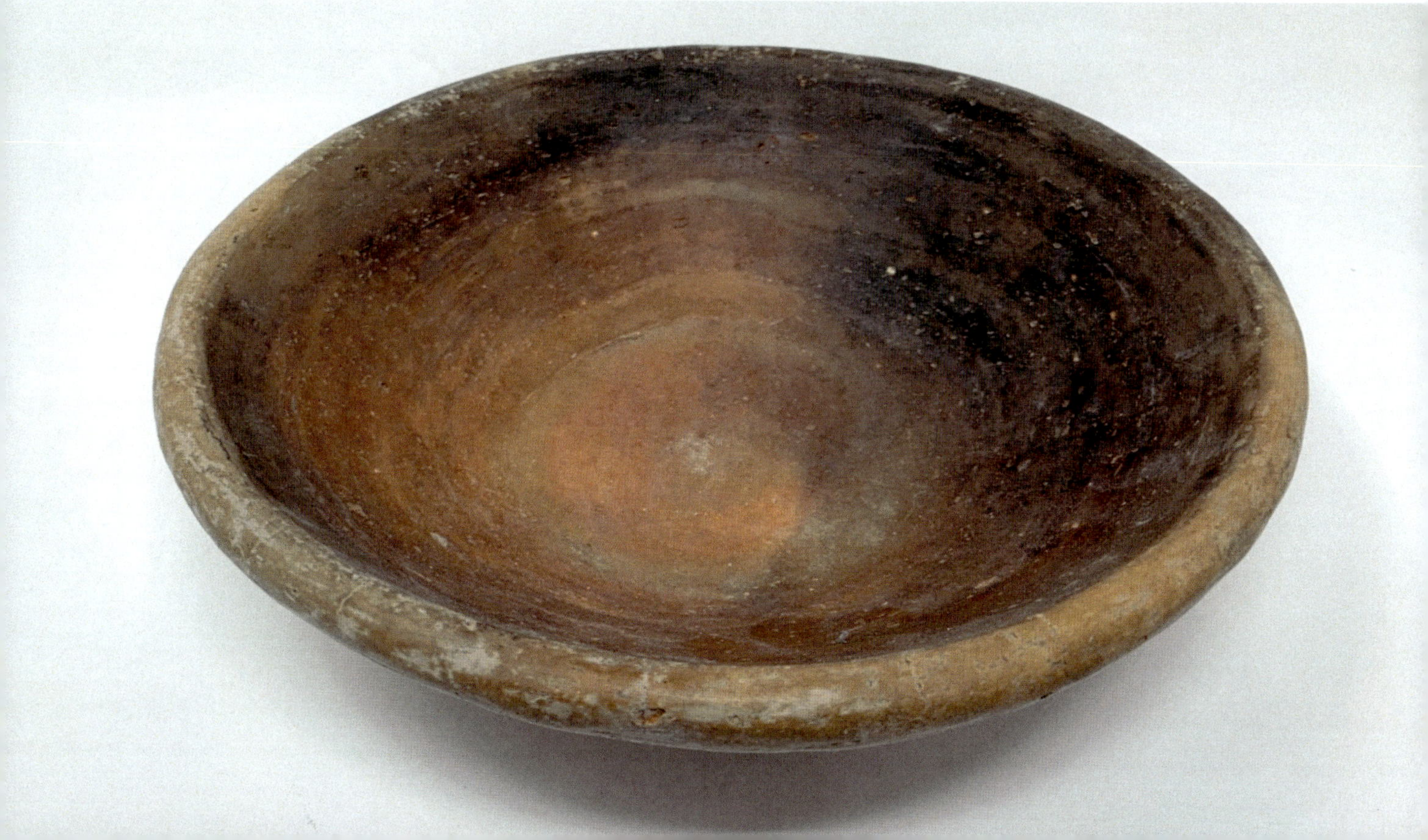

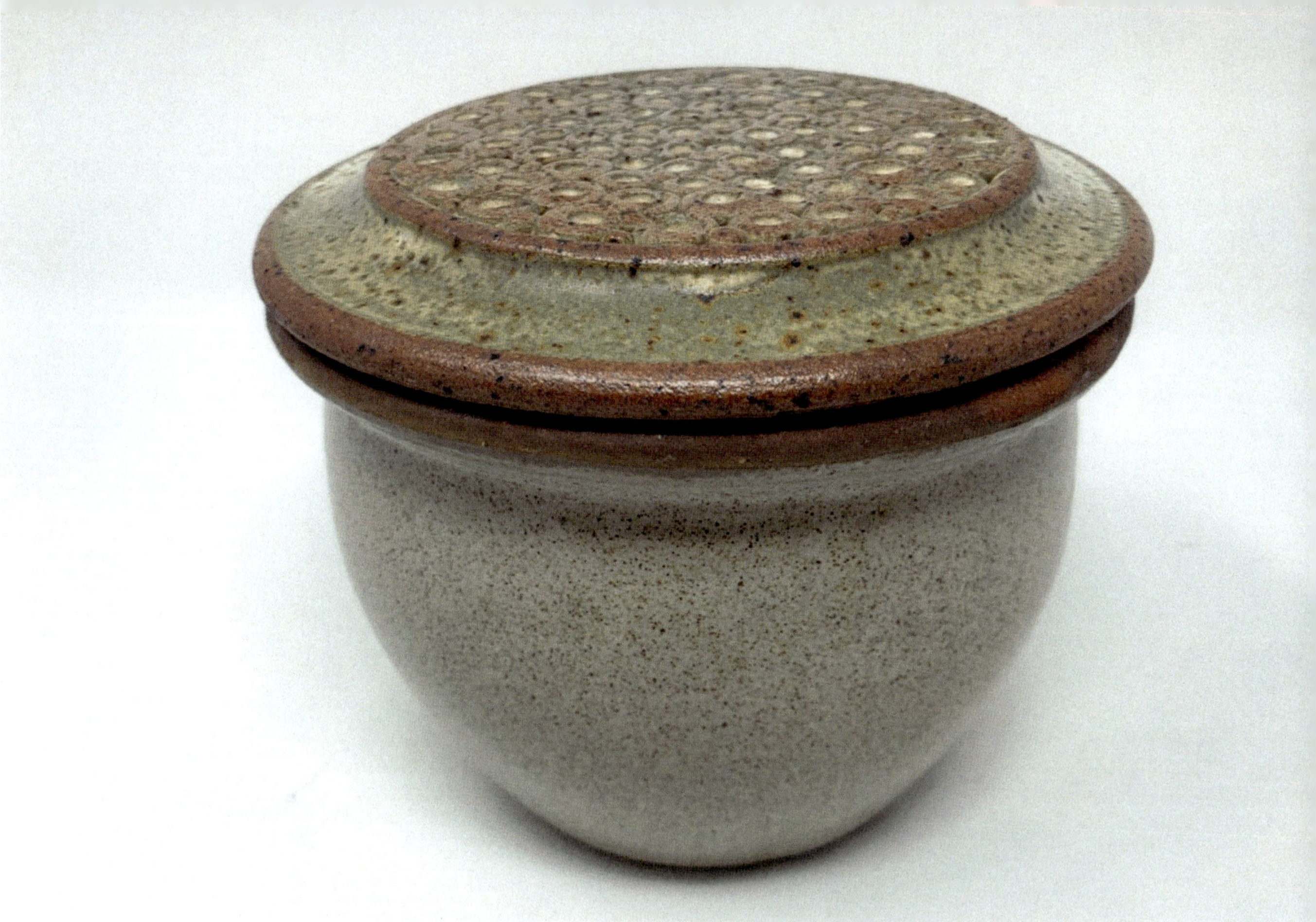

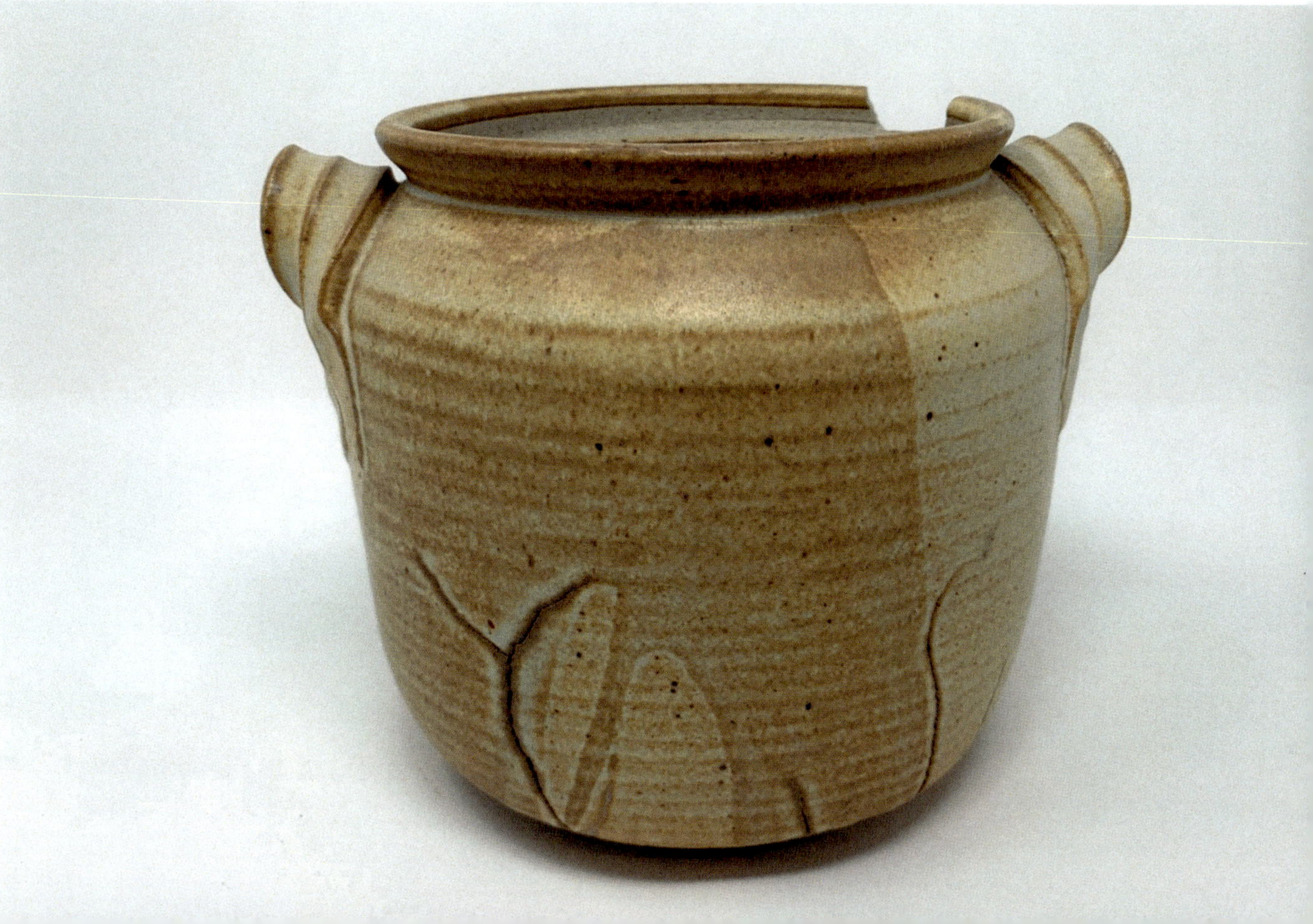

O God give me the
guidance to know
when to hold on
and when to let go
and give me the
grace 'ere also the
right decision at the
right time in the right
way with dignity
You have to
balance the weight against
the weight

Mary Borgstrom

TO THE RECIPIENT,
One does not know or at best cannot be sure what another is thinking or feeling. Not in the same way as hearing clearly, concisely what is being said.

One cannot see or hear when another is hurting, weary, saddened, rushed for time or disappointed with dashed hopes and broken promises. Surprisingly often, many of these Emotional negatives overwhelm a person like a snowstorm and one loses their perspective.

Solutions here might be to explain to your child – 'this is what is happening'.

But perhaps the Mother's instinct – the Parent in us is to protect, protect and shield the innocent, the innocence of the child and protect yourself from revealing your own imperfections – you don't have all the answers. You cannot do everything, you can't make everything right, you can't prevent all the bad things. You are just an ordinary average person. Not perfect – trying to create a perfect family. Trying to prepare a perfect future for them, teaching, correcting, informing and disciplining so they won't suffer the same mistakes you yourself made.

NOTE: It is possible that this is advice **to** Mary, rather than **from** Mary.

Mary Borgstrom

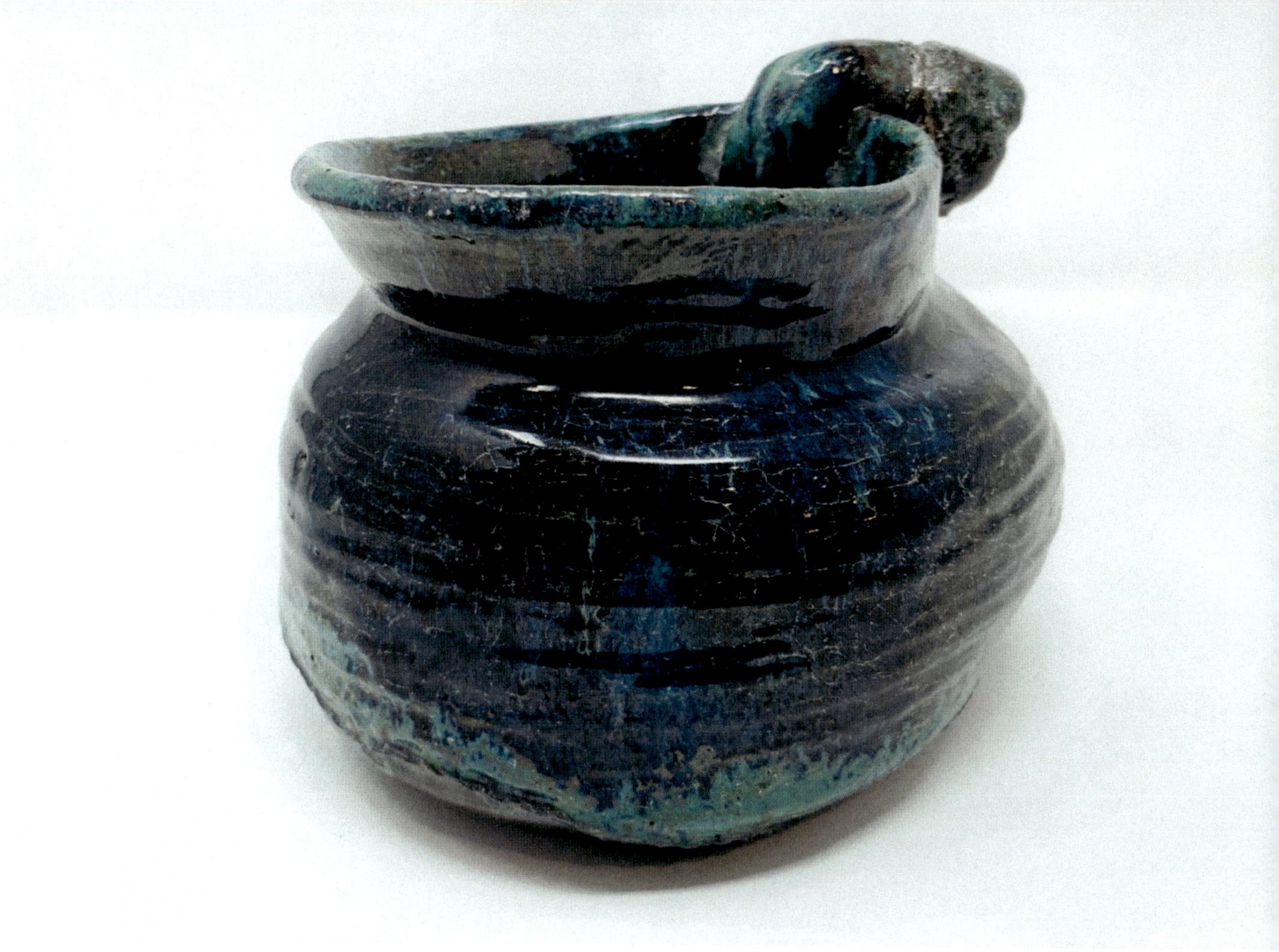

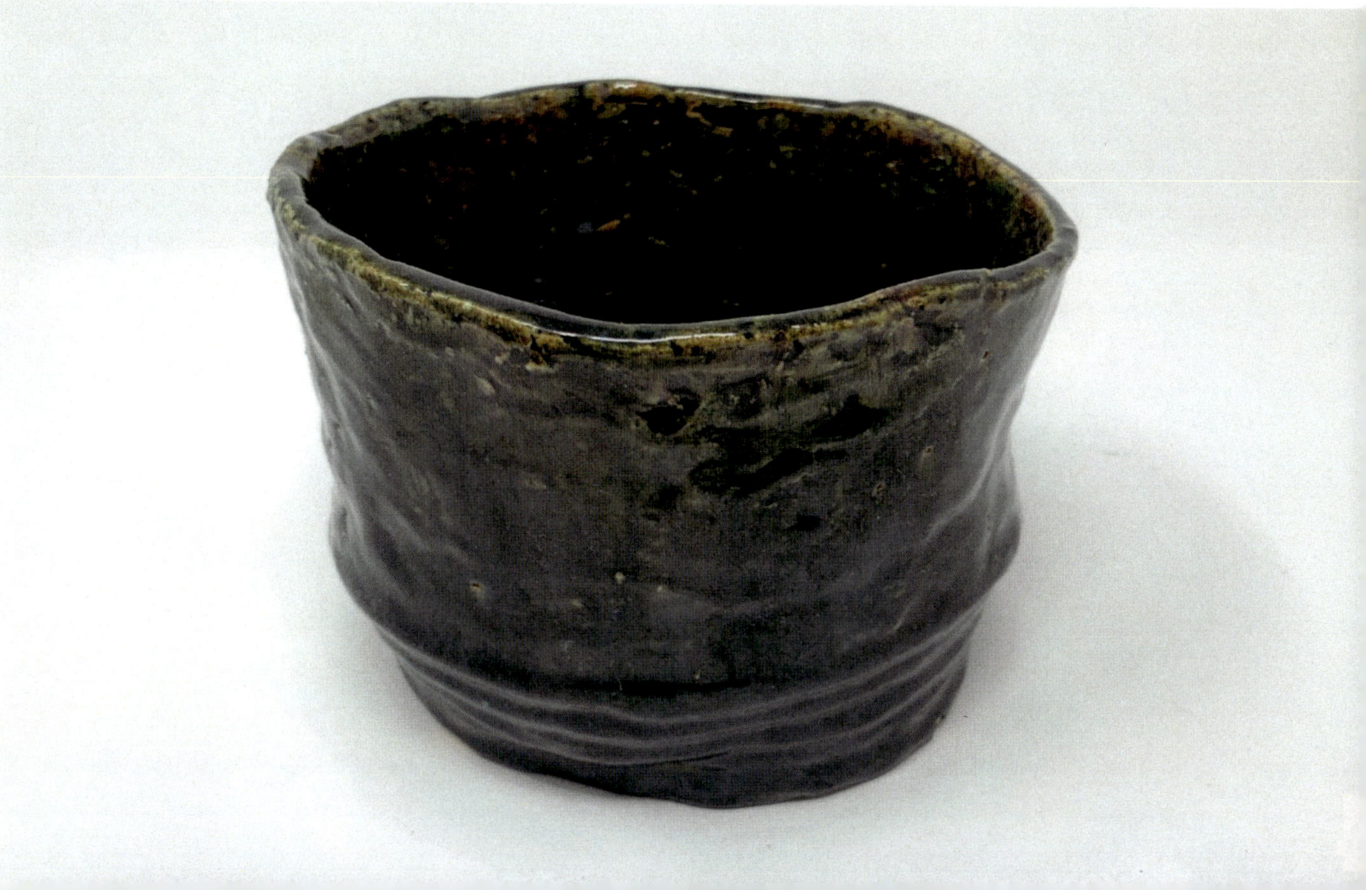

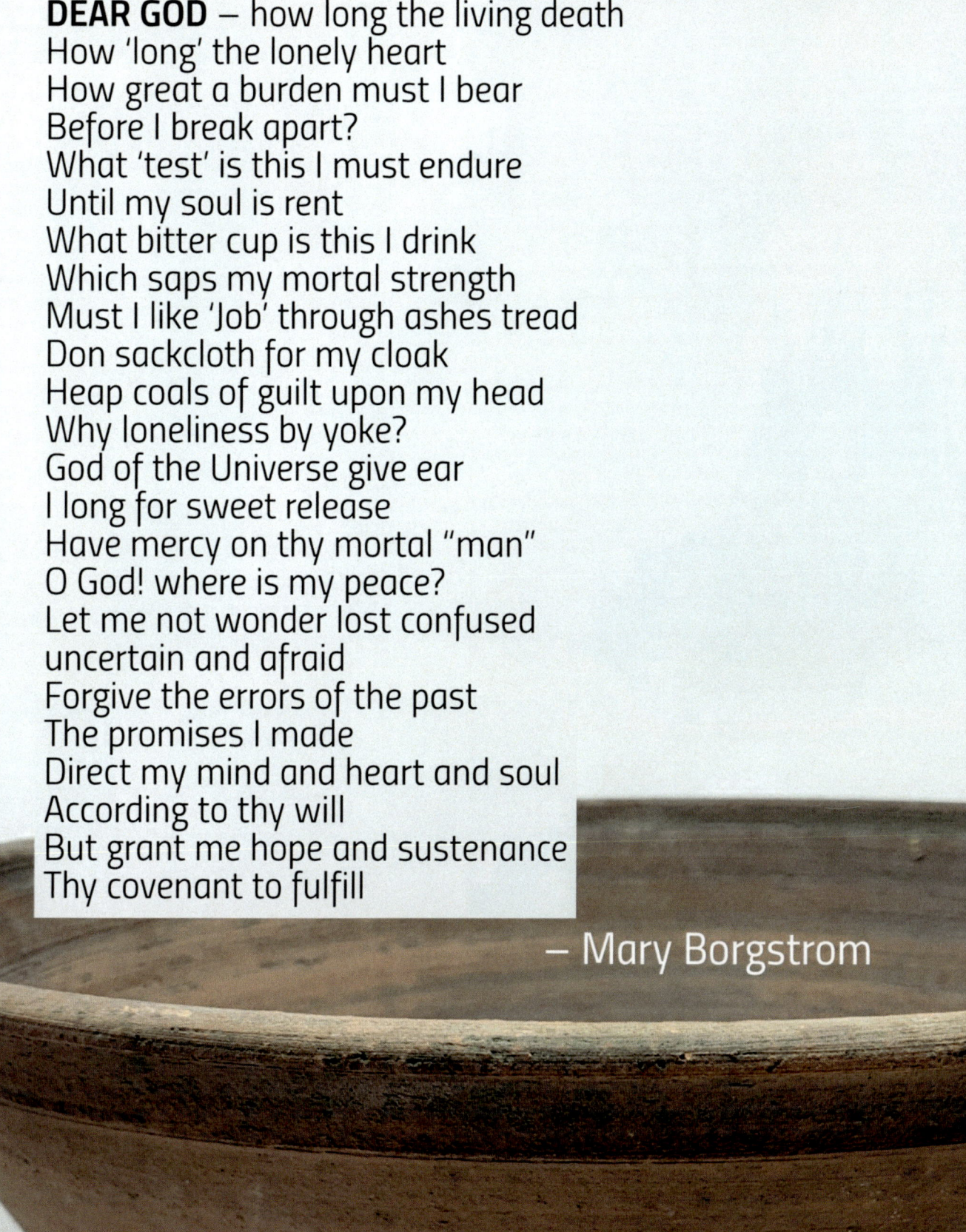

DEAR GOD – how long the living death
How 'long' the lonely heart
How great a burden must I bear
Before I break apart?
What 'test' is this I must endure
Until my soul is rent
What bitter cup is this I drink
Which saps my mortal strength
Must I like 'Job' through ashes tread
Don sackcloth for my cloak
Heap coals of guilt upon my head
Why loneliness by yoke?
God of the Universe give ear
I long for sweet release
Have mercy on thy mortal "man"
O God! where is my peace?
Let me not wonder lost confused
uncertain and afraid
Forgive the errors of the past
The promises I made
Direct my mind and heart and soul
According to thy will
But grant me hope and sustenance
Thy covenant to fulfill

– Mary Borgstrom

DEAR WAITING II

Dear Waiting – I read your poem to-day
How you watched for someone to come your way
How you planned to chat, perhaps serve tea
And I pictured how cozy this visit would be

When you heard the hesitant knock on your door
Your heart near 'stopped – afraid to explore
Then your eyes lit up and you stood so tall
"Please come on in – how nice of you to call"
Your face breaks into a radiant smile
"Please take this chair and do stay awhile,
Just give me a moment, some tea to prepare"
And you set the tray with infinite care

You glow from within as the two of you chatter
Of this that and the other – the topics no matter
Then the visit is over – must you go
Reluctant at parting – no longer aglow
So much left to say – when no one to listen
Softly closing the door – tear drops now glisten

Yes I read your poem to-day and
    I know what you mean
For you've stolen the lines
    of a well-rehearsed scene
From the everyday Drama of My Personal Play
    as I watch from my window day after day,
But it won't really happen I say through my tears
My day after day is a habit of years
But hope slowly dies and I can't help but wonder
If we indeed should meet
    of what 'lighting' and Thunder
as we visit and chatter – through laughter and tears
and call on each other making up for lost years.

Mary Borgstrom

REGARDING FAMILY RELATIONSHIPS

All members of the family, and family, including our son and daughter, have been and always will be dearly loved. Not for what they are, who they are. They are loved because they are family.

Any problems/friction between me and a family member should be just that. It is our private responsibility to repair or adjust that problem, simply because it is we two who are involved. If the family en masse – jumps into the fray we escalate the problem and keep it alive. Fanning the Flame so to speak and adding fuel with dialogue, attitude and action. The two involved do not solve their problem. The mass comes to a decision and legislated a court order of sorts. Like only these two can resolve their love and friendship it cannot be forced. It has to be allowed to progress naturally. A court order becomes a rule or Law outwardly. Resentment still flourishes underneath the surface.

— Mary Borgstrom

Those times when the mind and soul become destitute and desperate, subconsciously calling out for help.

STRENGTH

What is strength?

I believe strength is derived from effort to overcome weaknesses and problems. Each success of effort to overcome Strength is built up and fortified, thus hope and fortitude is built and rebuilt into permanent lasting strength.

— Mary Borgstrom

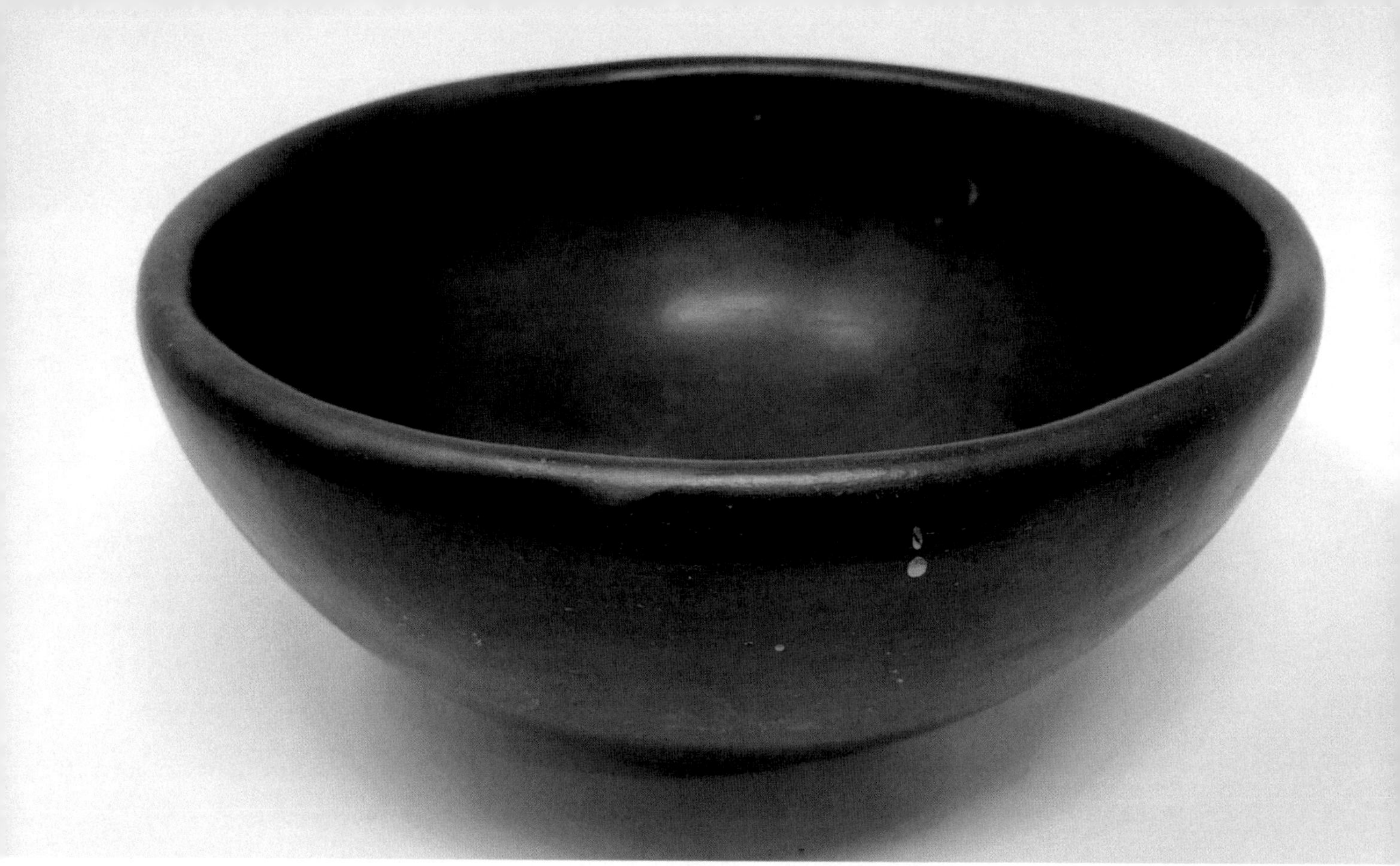

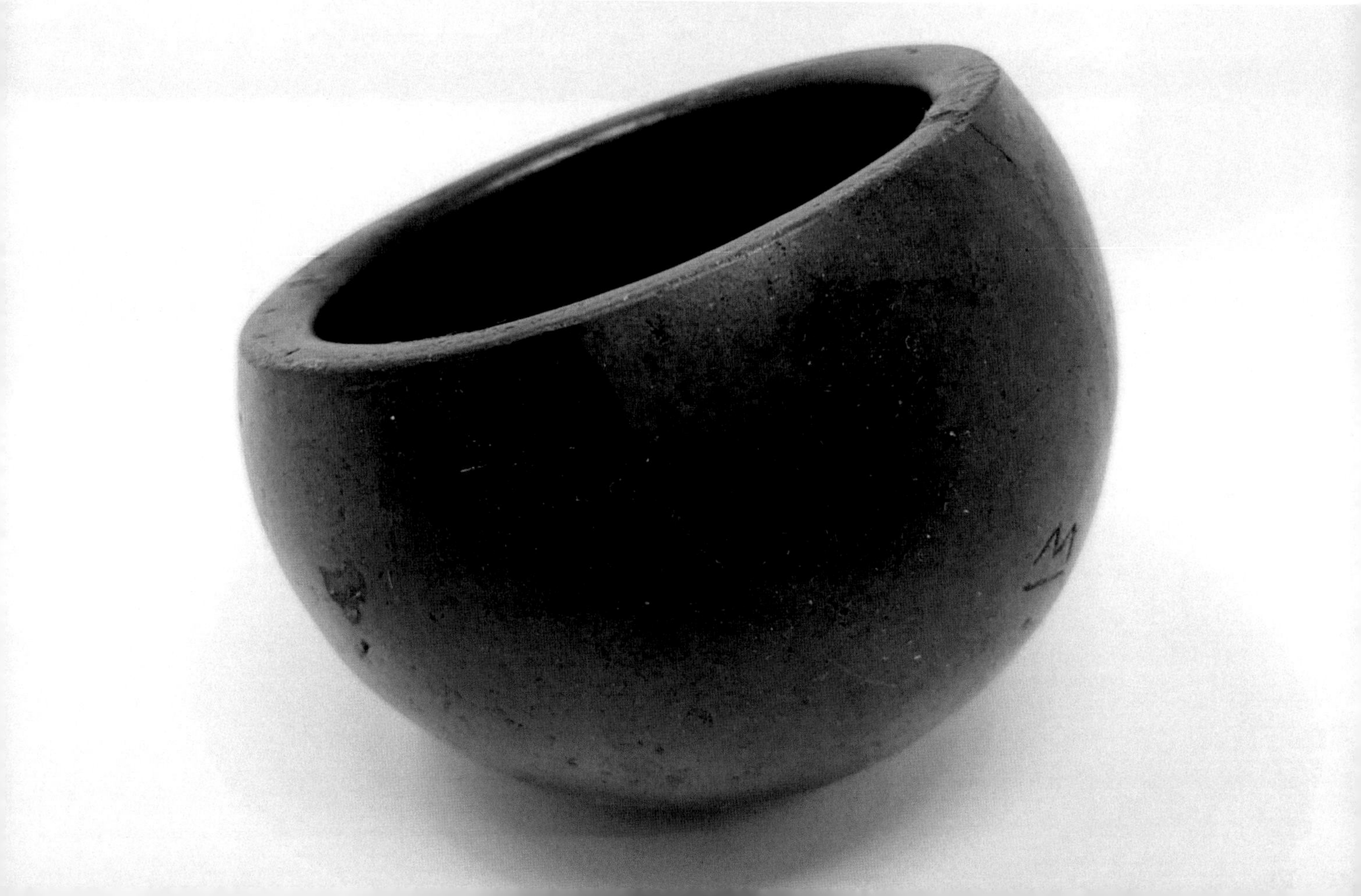

You restored strength when strength seemed gone
You made me whole when I was torn
You gave me hope perhaps in vain
you dried my tears I smiled again
You set my feet to walk once more
Nominee the trials and the stones now sharp no more
So his excelled you may be
towards the distant rock strewn shore
A world apart from these and me
A tongue unknown – a world not mine
A breathless pause in realms of time
I crossed the threshold stepped inside
Thought but to linger and hide
But when I left my lost soul cried
Twas but a moment, brief and eternal.
Perhaps you guessed by grief infernal
Yet how to know
How could you know the depths and hollows
The tears unshed, the hearts keep wallows
I glimpsed of a world not mine, not theirs
Nor even yours
Though you at least have found a measure of belonging
You too are seeking to assuage
For footholds that prove lasting
the restoration you too are searching, seeking
Perhaps tis why we knew not why
and understood heard the cry so deep within
and unbeknown and without plan
we touched this chord of fellowman
Knowing not what depths or measure
we shared a precious priceless treasure
gave of ourselves, a priceless treasure

**You did not know nor could you guess
of a Life time stress.**

Mary Borgstrom

THE COCOON OF WINTER'S SNOW

From within winter's cocoon of snow
Emerges adolescent spring
Bedecked with flowers of every hue
Against a background of virgin greens
Spotlighted by the heat of Sun
Surrounded by the blistering Sun
Highlighted by Sun's radiant light
and so we welcome the radiant bride
   of summer

Mary Borgstrom

Just a word, Just a line
To say I'm glad that you are mine
The happiness which fills my soul
Enlist me in the "lover's role"

Mary Borgstrom

Wondered pearl
on granite sea
shakily
the tide that
rose warm
and red in
evening sun-
swept to shore
the mocking
sand harsh
and cold white
foam licking
bright and
glowing moon
washed star
flecked and
scrunched by
feet the downing rose.

Mary Borgstrom

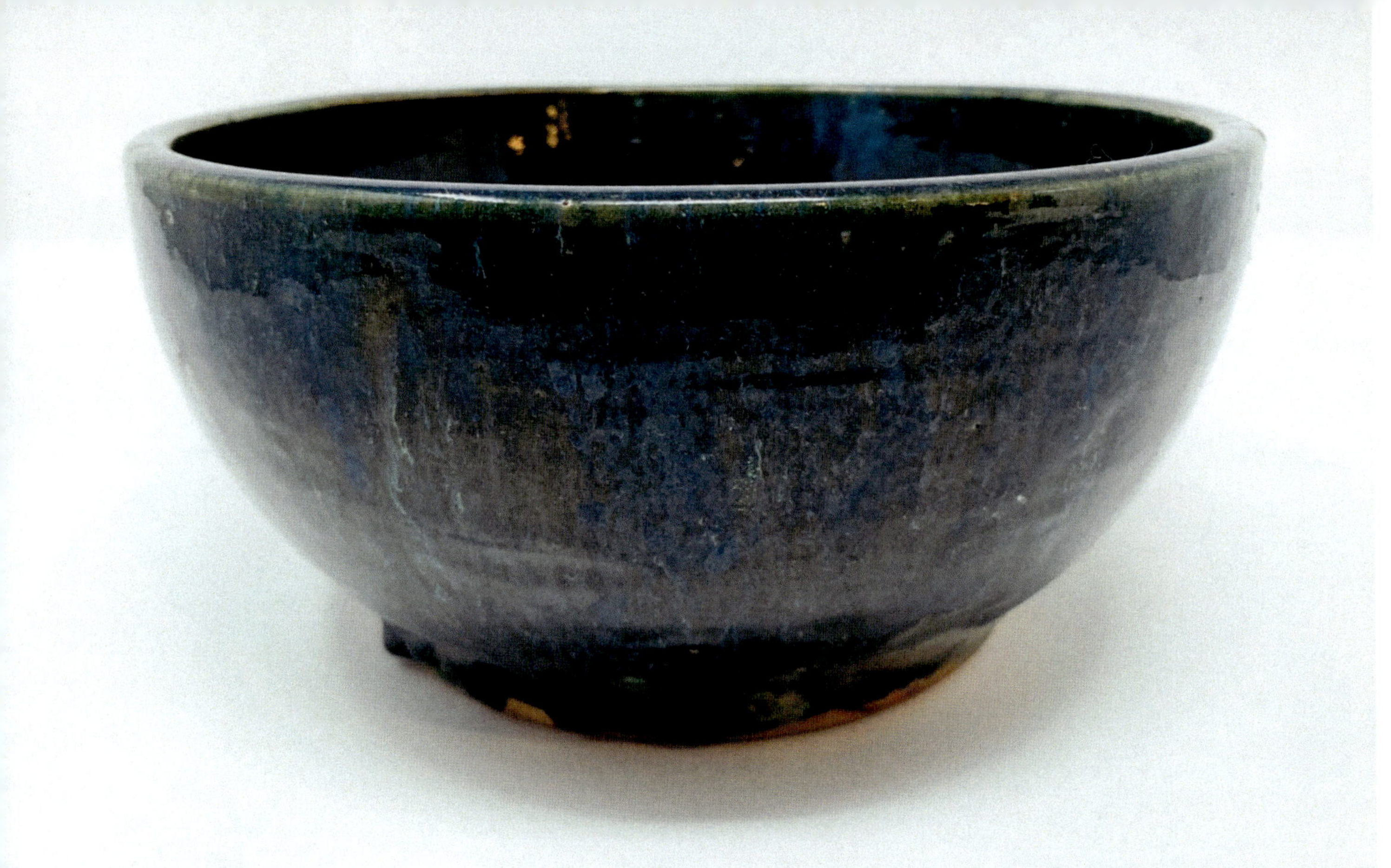

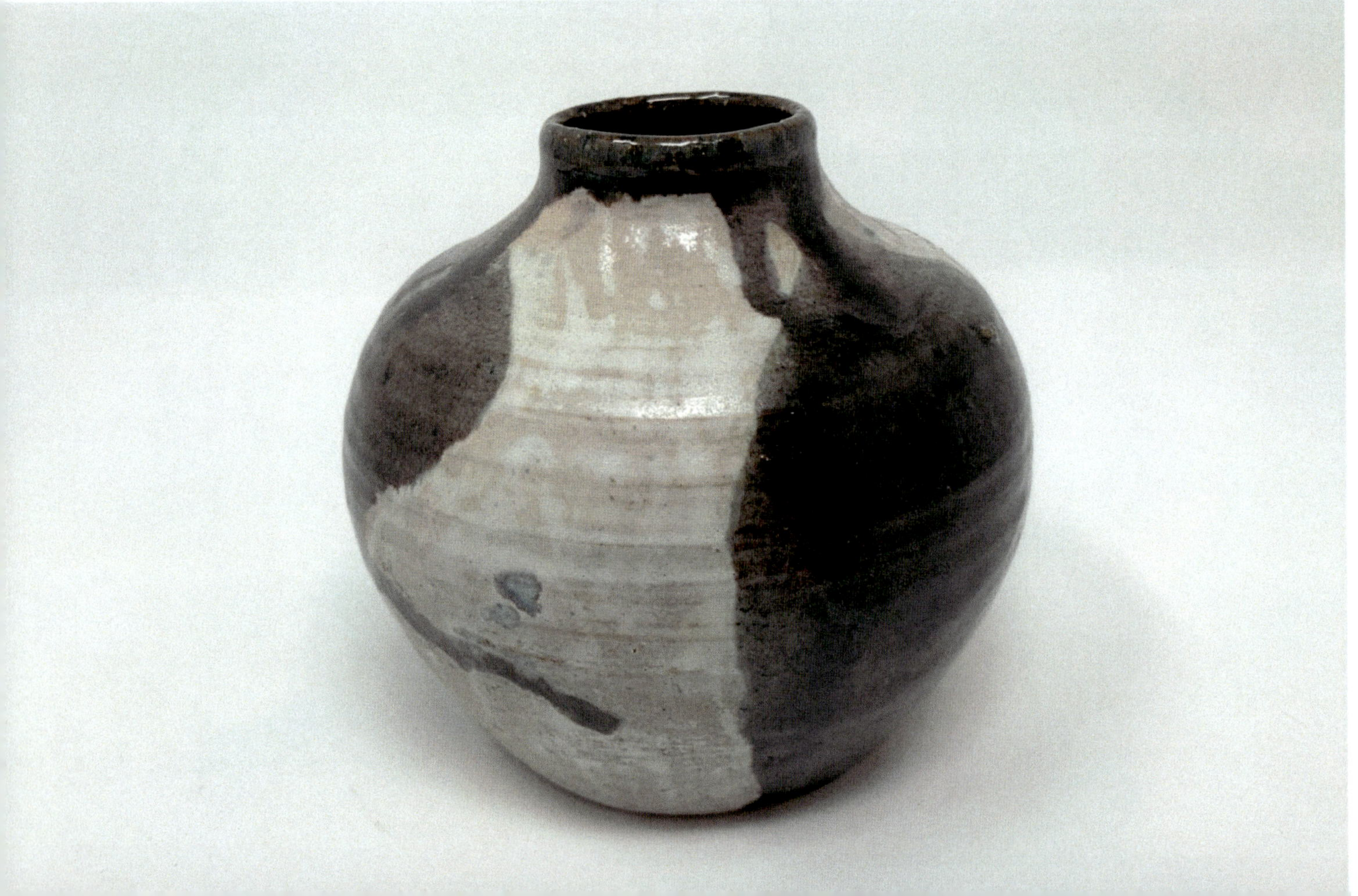

PERHAPS!

I check my life in Retrospect
Perhaps to find a key
That might unlock another door
Where I have hidden me
A time span of four score and more
In life's ever changing scene
Gives but a fleeting threshold glimpse
of all that life should mean
Comprehension, Tolerance, Truth,
Love for Fellow-man
Demands wisdom beyond this life now
A bridge I cannot span
Perhaps I'll understand
Why I am me — no more — no less
In God's Eternal Plan.
And so Perhaps I should not dwell
on inconsequential me
Just live each day the Simple Life.

THE POTTER'S HOUSE

Here are some pictures of the Potter's House, both in-progress and completed. This book focused on Mary Borgstrom's art and poetry found in the process of restoring her former home. To see the actual process of the renovations, as well as the rest of the series, visit the *Curiosity Incorporated* YouTube channel.

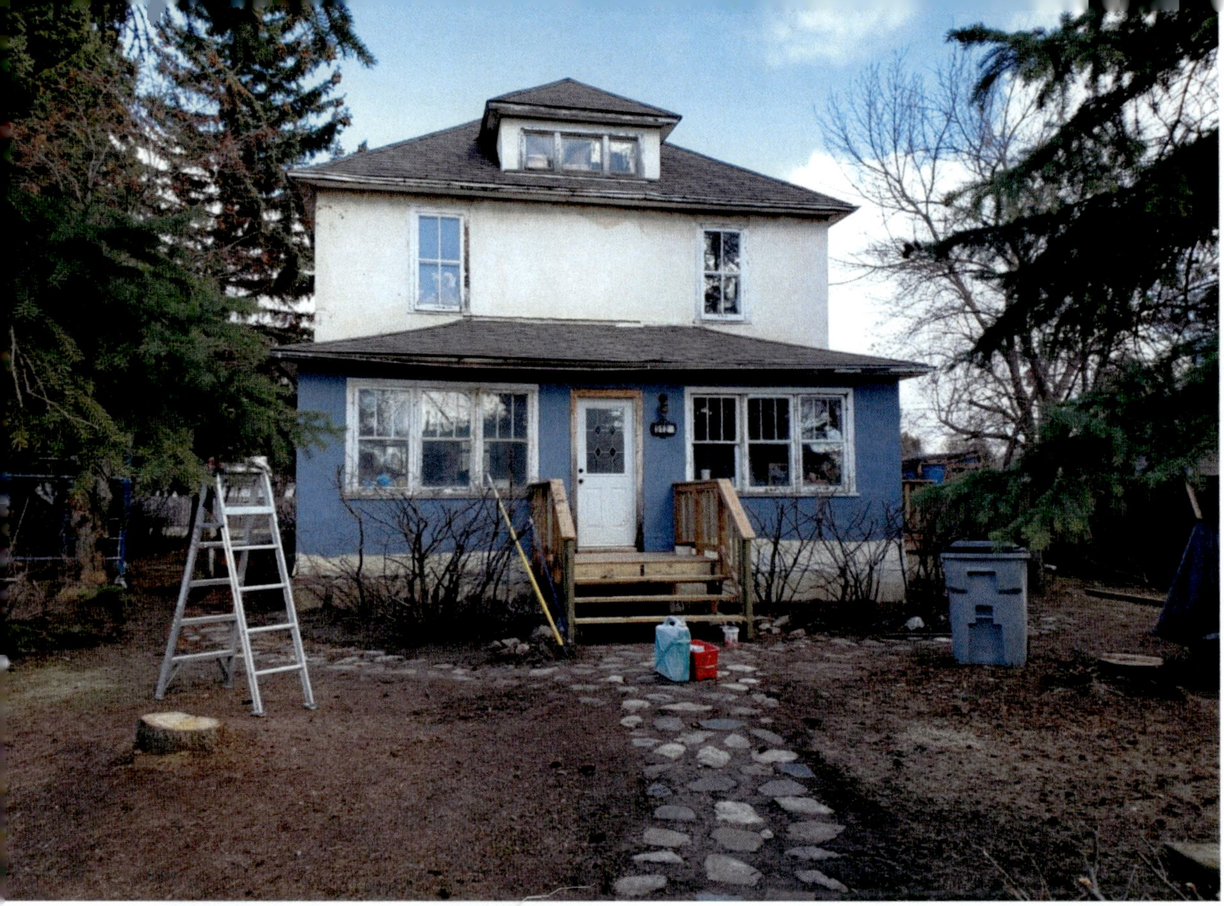

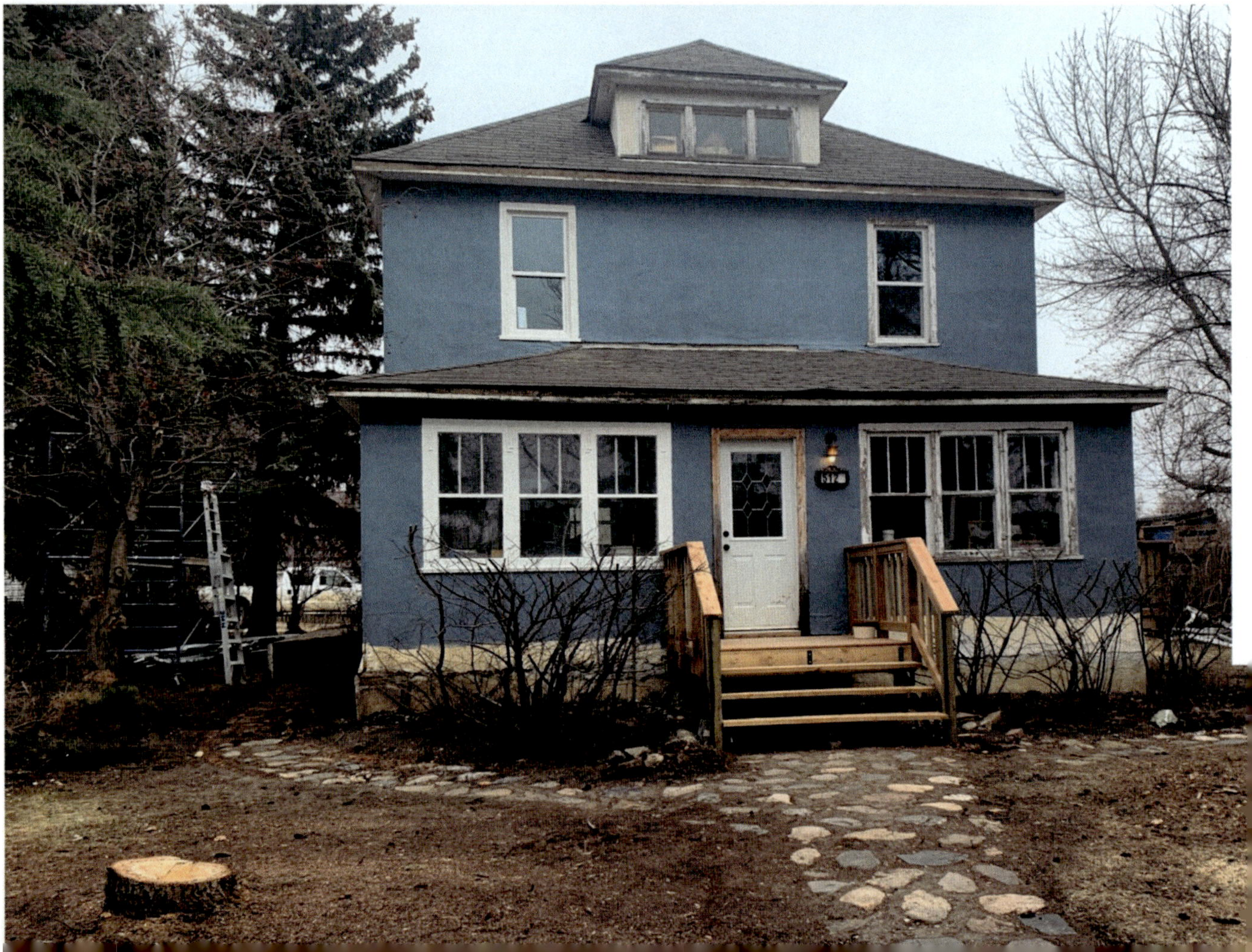
512

FRONT
OF THE HOUSE

FRONT
PORCH/SUNROOM

DINING ROOM
& SITTING AREA

KITCHEN

FORMAL LIVING ROOM

STAIRS
OFF SITTING AREA

UPSTAIRS
BATHROOM

ADDITIONAL ROOM
WITH HIDDEN ACCESS TO ATTIC

MASTER
BEDROOM

GUEST
BEDROOM

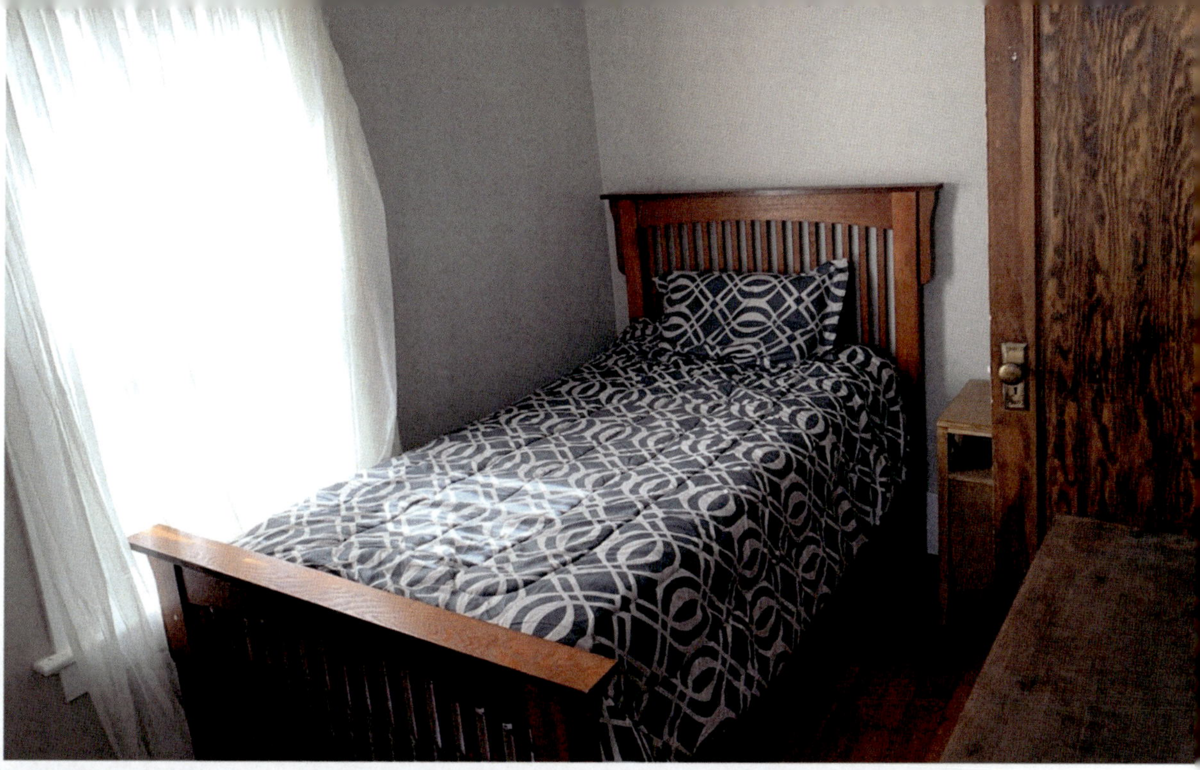

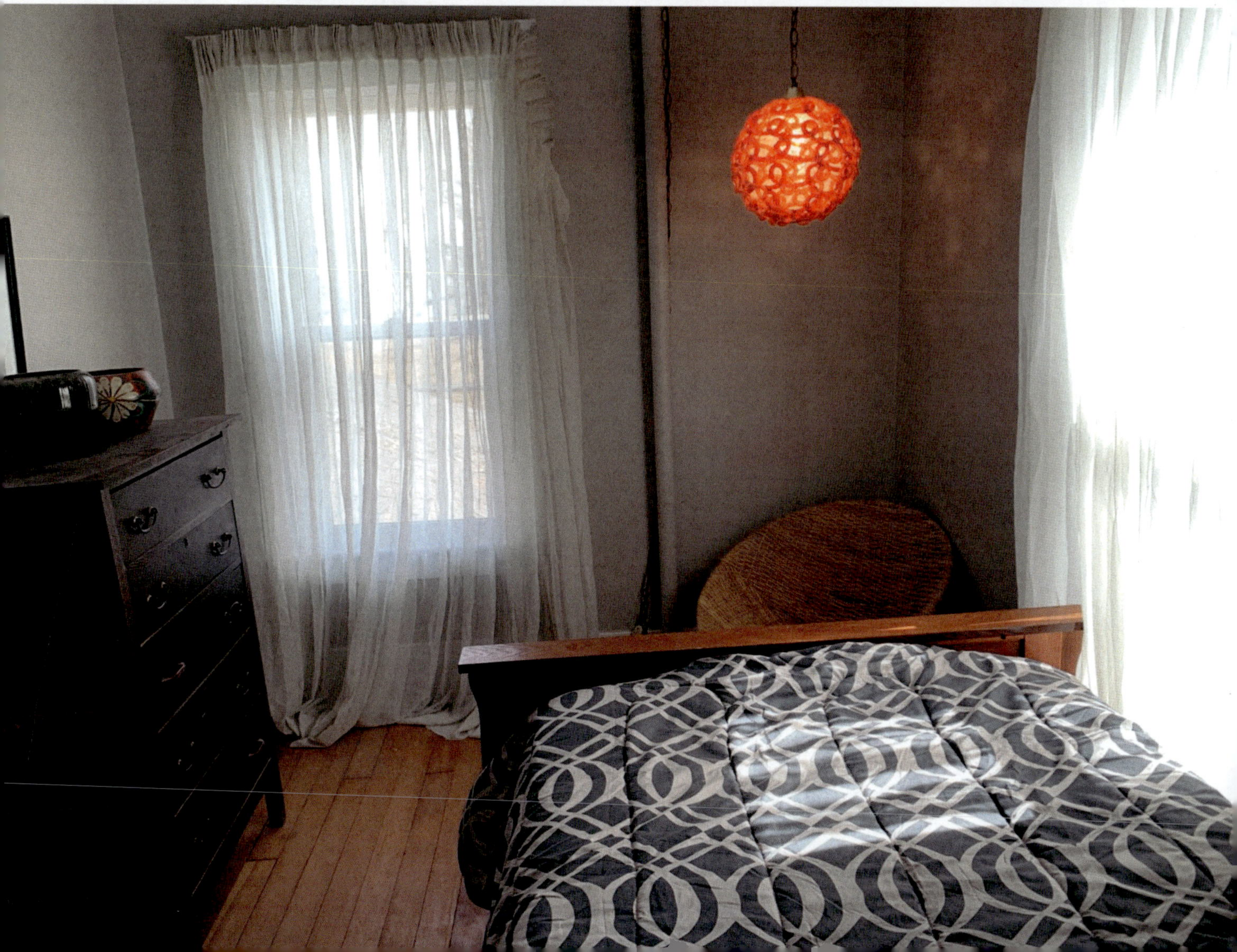

On the first weekend of April in 2019, Alex had planned to take Mary to see the house. Most of the major parts of the renovation had been or were near completion. It was a chance to let Mary see her former home as it was so many years ago.

Unfortunately, it was not meant to be.

On April 3rd, 2019, Mary passed away in the town she had come to call home, Provost. She was 102 years old.

She never got to see the house, renovated, in person.

But maybe... just maybe... Mary felt that her house – her home – and her legacy was in good hands. And maybe, just maybe, she felt comfortable enough to pass on to the other side and satisfy her curiosity of what was waiting for her there.

One of her last requests was to have her final ride in Curiosity Inc.'s *Ghostbusters* ambulance. Alex was more than happy to honor the request. The funeral procession drove by Mary's house with the ambulance's lights and sirens on, marking her final visit to the place she had called home for so many years, and the end of a long journey.

HERE/AFTER

Those of us who fear Life's Close
And wonder – why this mystery
Searching answers – since our Birth
Find no revealing history

One thing we know without dispute
Death comes to all – making claim
With measured steps, oft unannounced
Presents the card with Someone's name

But rest assured God is aware
of the manner, time and place
Life of Man is God's mandate
Tempered with His Grace

The timing will be God's own time
His wisdom makes the rules.
Those who think they have a choice
Indulge the thoughts of fools

Man has no miracles of his own
To stay the Tides of Time
Not by one wit – extend his days
Or – hold man in his prime.

Why not, reach out and take God's hand
In your journey toward the unknown
And when you breath Life's final Breath
You need not – will not – walk alone.

Mary Borgstrom

Painting of the Potter's House by Alex's mother, Lynda

MAY 18th, 1916
—
APRIL 3rd, 2019

Mary Borgstrom

ALEXANDER ARCHBOLD and his wife, Melissa, opened *Curiosity Inc.*, an antiques store, in Edmonton, Alberta, Canada in 2016. After working in the film and retail industries, Alex wanted to spend more time with his family and friends, going on adventures and finding amazing things. In 2017, Alex started a YouTube channel to share these adventures with the world.

Watch the entire **Potter's House** series on *Curiosity Incorporated*'s YouTube channel.

Visit them on:
Instagram (@curiosityincyeg)
Facebook (Curiosity Incorporated)
www.curiosityedmonton.ca

Made in the USA
Middletown, DE
20 March 2020